astle

Architect Royal

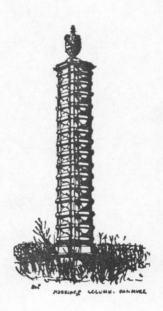

Marriage Column, Panmure

Sir William Bruce of Kinross, Bart. Portrait by John Michael Wright at Kinross.

Architect Royal

The Life and Works of
Sir William Bruce
1630 – 1710

Hubert Fenwick

A.R.I.B.A.

Kineton : The Roundwood Press

1970

SBN 900093 12 9

Set in 'Monotype' Bell, series 341 and printed by Gordon Norwood at
The Roundwood Press, Kineton, in the County of Warwick.
Plates made by The Process Engraving Company Limited, Coventry.
Lithography by Charles Hill of Warwick.

Made and printed in Great Britain

Architecture has really one means: proportion, proportion of space. As an art, architecture is just as immaterial as any other form of art, because its significance is not in its material but in its spiritual value, namely in how the architect has managed to express an idea in terms of spatial relationship. This is a value extending beyond time, which raises architecture above the change of fashion.

w. m. DUDOCK in the course of a letter to the President of the R.I.B.A. in response to a congratulatory epistle from that body on the occasion of his 80th birthday in July 1964.

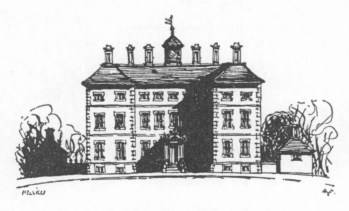

Melville (original design)

Doocot, Kinross

Contents

Illustrations

Acknowledgments

THE AUTHOR AND PUBLISHERS wish to thank H.M. The Queen for gracious permission to reproduce the following photographs in this book; plates 32, 33, 34 and 35; and the Marquis of Linlithgow by whose courtesy plates 91 and 92 appear. Thanks are also due to the Earl of Haddington for permission to reproduce plate 76; the National Portrait Gallery for plates 1 and 2; the Tate Gallery for plate 7; and the National Galleries of Scotland for plates 8 and 95. Plates 13, 14, 21, 22, 38, 40, 54, 56 and 83 are reproduced by courtesy of the National Monuments Record of Scotland; plates 90, 93 and 94 by that of John Dewar, and plates 51, 52, 53, 55, 73, 75 and 77 of Tom Scott. The coloured frontispiece was specially taken by Douglas Gray of Park Film Studios, Glasgow, by kind permission of Mrs P. R. Montgomery. The sketches and, except where otherwise stated, the rest of the photographs, are all by the author.

North facade; Balcaskie

Craftsmen at Holyrood, circa 1680

Foreword

I AM DELIGHTED to have been asked by the author to write a foreword to this book.

I have been in fairly close contact with him since he undertook some years ago the restoration of the unique Bruce aisle and family 'loft' in Abercorn Church.

Of Bruce as a man little is known, but there is enough to recognise in him a man of intense loyalties and integrity, who suffered for his political convictions and exerted an important influence upon the political events of his time.

In this context I cannot go all the way with the author who places Bruce in Scotland except for occasional visits to the Continent, during the Commonwealth period. It has been a traditional belief of my family, the Hopes of Hopetoun, that Bruce spent most of those years exiled in Holland. Certainly his style of architecture owed much to continental influence, and we know that he employed Dutch craftsmen to carry out much of his work after the Restoration.

As significant perhaps is the wording of the 'laissez passer' for Bruce signed by General Monk and referred to in this book. The reader will notice the phrase 'until his *return* into Holland'. He must also have been well known to Charles II, since honours and royal commissions flowed upon him after the Restoration. I think it most likely that Bruce offered his services to Charles as a mediator with the powerful Monk, rather than the other way round. Bruce's close association with the Royal House is again emphasised by his fall from favour and imprisonment after the 1688 revolution.

As an architect he has I believe been very underestimated. It was his good fortune to reach maturity exactly at the right moment. The junction of the thrones of Scotland and England had opened up to the remarkable native talents of Scotland a whole range of influences and activities hitherto suppressed by self centred squabbles and a certain provincial exclusiveness.

These events were closely reflected in the rise of a new type of Scottish lowland laird, prosperous and canny but with expanded views of comfort and culture. Not for them the ancient Keeps and drafty Peel Towers of their predecessors. They required restrained and practical mansions, not too grand for their purses, but grand enough to reflect their exalted stations in a thrusting and adventurous community. Bruce supplied them for others, and for himself.

Bruce was too early for the great flood of Italian and Palladian influences on English and Scottish domestic architecture. It was left to another Fife family, William Adam and his sons, to exploit these some 30 years later, but it is a happy thing for posterity that this was so. It makes Bruce unique and his houses particularly Scottish and peculiarly his own. Living as my family has done in a Bruce House later embellished by William Adam and his sons, one likes to believe one has the best of both worlds – but I sometimes wonder.

LINLITHGOW

West front, Hopetoun

Introduction

THE LATE Mr David Marshall, in notes published by the Society
of Antiquaries in Scotland (Volume 14), likened Sir William
Bruce of Kinross, Bart, (the first Scottish architect in modern
terms), to Inigo Jones (the first English architect), and with some
justification, as we shall see. Mr Marshall also, curiously enough,
ended his notes with the hope that someone else might use them as
the basis for a book on Bruce, which he says, he had hoped to write
himself but had been prevented from doing for a number of reasons,
but principally through lack of a knowledge of architecture. He did
accomplish a most valuable work, however, in sorting out the contents of the Charter Room at Kinross House and reading through the
relevant correspondence and accounts. A difficult task as anyone
will know who has tried to decipher centuries old letters and bills.
The fruits of these worthy labours appeared first in a lecture on
Kinross-shire, in general, and Kinross House, in particular, which
David Marshall gave in 1881, and which formed the bulk of the
material later deposited with the Society of Antiquaries and now
housed in the Register House in Edinburgh. Marshall's researches,
plus letters once in the possession of the Bruces of Arnot (now
defunct), and the interesting papers of the Mylne family of masons
(Robert Mylne built most of the Palace of Holyroodhouse for
Charles II under Sir William Bruce's surveillance), are what I have
chiefly built my narrative upon. I only hope I have lived up to his
expectations, voiced many years ago.

Bruce was, in truth, the 'Scottish Inigo Jones,' though Daniel
Defoe, writing in his *Tour thro' the whole Island of Great Britain*,
refers to him as the 'Kit Wren of Scotland,' and goes on to describe
Bruce's house, at Kinross, as 'the most beautiful (for a Gentleman's
Seat), in the Kingdom.' — an opinion which will be shared by many
today. The fact is, of course, that Bruce was both the Scottish Wren
and the Scottish Inigo Jones, 'The introducer of Architecture in this
country,' as Sir John Clerk of Penicuik said. With Wren too he was
encouraged in the practice of the 'Mistress Art' by a perspicacious

'Merry Monarch,' who created him Surveyor of Public Works in Scotland, France and Ireland, a post held in England by the man who designed St. Paul's Cathedral and Chelsea Hospital.

William Bruce was the second son of Robert Bruce of Blairhall, in Fife, an ancestor of the present Earl of Elgin and Kincardine. The precise date of his birth is uncertain but it was sometime in 1630. The period was a troubled one and this may account for discrepancies in recorded detail. It may also account for a similar haziness as to the exact place and time of Bruce's death, which is generally supposed to have occurred at Kinross, early in the year 1710. He was a staunch episcopalian and loyal subject of the native line of kings, and was thrice jailed for his beliefs. On the first occasion, in 1693, his wife, Mary Halket of Pitfirrane, voluntarily shared his imprisonment, dying three years afterwards. Bruce then remarried. The second Lady Bruce, born Magdalen Scott, was what is commonly called a 'character.' She survived her husband by more than forty years and was alive in 1752; which certainly disproves any theories that our architect remarried again. It also bears out the possibility of Lady Bruce having made contact with the famous Flora MacDonald, which she is said to have done, whilst that Jacobite heroine was at Leith, *en route* for London and the Tower.

Though renowned as an architect Bruce began his career in the political field. It appears that in 1658, when Cromwell died, the youthful William Bruce decided to make it his business to become acquainted with General Monk and try and persuade that key personage to offer his sword to the King, then in exile in Holland. The plan seems to have succeeded for Monk sent Bruce across to the Continent as his envoy, permitting him to keep his sword 'until he returned into Holland,' as the passport, dated September 7th, 1659, and signed by the General himself, states. At the Restoration, when Monk was made a Duke for his decisive action in marching with the Coldstream Guards to London, Bruce became Clerk to the Bills, a lucrative appointment by which he received a fee on every measure passed by the Scottish Parliament. Other official posts followed, notably that of Surveyor to the King's Works; and in 1668 he was created a Baronet of Nova Scotia with title to Balcaskie, in Fife. He afterwards bought the Kinross Estate, and as the result of a letter from Charles II to his brother James, Duke of York, he became Parliamentary Representative and High Sheriff of "Kinrosher". With the fall of the House of Stewart, however, in 1688, his days in the public service were numbered. He resigned his offices, and was taken into protective custody.

It is virtually impossible to say for certain where or when Sir William Bruce learnt the art of architecture, least of all how, except by keen observation and by the practice of much trial and error. He obviously had a considerable natural gift, but unlike Inigo Jones he was not sent to Italy at royal expense to study the works of Palladio in the flesh; though he clearly made good use of his oppportunities during the last years of the Cromwellian dictatorship when he went abroad at Monk's behest. Letters between him and the Duke of Lauderdale (his patron in later years) also mention personal favours done by Bruce in searching out *objets d'art* in Holland and France; and this collecting he developed more between 1660 and 1671, when he was appointed King's Surveyor and Architect for the rebuilding of Holyroodhouse. The terraces at Balcaskie exhibit in the most vivid manner imaginable what excellent use Bruce made of his travels abroad to improve his knowledge of formal landscaping and to acquire busts, statues and urns not only for Lauderdale but for himself. The reshaping of Balcaskie house too, represents a series of experimental architectural exercises undertaken in the days before he obtained important contracts from the King's Commissioner in Scotland.

Mr David Marshall attempted a list of Bruce's complete works, some of them authentic, some not. They included, besides Holyrood and other well known public enterprises, Balcaskie, Thirlestane, Kinross, much of Hopetoun, Harden (now called Mertoun) and Auchendinny. The present owners of these have shown a remarkably kind and lively interest in my efforts to carry on where Marshall left off, and without exception are very proud and happy to inhabit and possess homes designed by the first, and possibly the most interesting Scottish architect. Marshall's list also named a number of buildings associated with Bruce but not positively proved to have been his, such as Caroline Park, near Edinburgh, and Drumlanrig Castle, in Dumfriesshire, though the *Dictionary of National Biography* claims Drumlanrig for Colen Campbell.

When Bruce died, in 1710, his last big scheme, the House of Nairne, in Perthshire, had just been finished, but the family were Jacobites and their property was subsequently sold and the house deliberately burnt down. Thus the last remaining design by the former architect to Charles II is now the Laird's Loft, or Gallery, and Burial Aisle at Abercorn Kirk, in West Lothian; completed for the first Earl of Hopetoun in 1708, when Bruce was in his seventy-eighth year. I feel privileged to have assisted in the recent restoration of this unique architectural grouping. The restitution of so splendid an ensemble of Scottish, indeed British baroque art should serve as a small, if belated tribute to the 'Scottish Inigo Jones' who was also the 'Kit Wren of Scotland,' the man who may be said to have headed the movement which counted amongst its followers William Adam and sons, James Gibbs, Sir William Chambers and Charles Cameron (architect to Catherine the Great).

The Tzarina described Cameron as: 'Ecossais de nation, Jacobite de proféssion, grand dessinateur.' She might equally well have described him as the Kit Wren of Russia. Sacherverell Sitwell, in his *British Architects and Crafstmen*, says 'James Gibbs was a Scot, and, together with Charles Cameron and the brothers Adam, is probably, among the only artists of his race. All three are architects, and, perhaps, greater men than Raeburn, Scott or Robert Burns.' A contentious and provocative statement, which, however, contains a grain of truth; though it is odd there is no mention of either William Adam or Sir William Bruce, the latter does not even appear in the index. The *Dictionary of National Biography* is more generous, and adds, after commenting on Bruce's architectural exploits, a reference to the fact that in the political field the first Scottish architect probably did more, in a private capacity, to help bring about the Restoration of 1660 than anyone else in Scotland.

Raith, Kirkcaldy (conjectural restoration)

CHAPTER ONE

Early background

S IR WILLIAM BRUCE of Kinross, Bart., architect to Charles II, was descended from semi-royal ancestors, having Thomas Bruce, a cousin of Robert the Bruce, as ancestor. Together with Walter the Steward, afterwards the first Stewart King of Scots, Thomas Bruce assisted in the defence of his country against the English in 1334, and was rewarded for his services with a portion of the royal property in Clackmannanshire. Succeeding Bruces living in the country were styled 'of Clackmannan,' until the sixteenth century, when David Bruce resigned his rights to his uncle, Sir David Bruce of that Ilk, whom James IV had knighted. Thenceforth a new line branched off, to become extinct in 1912 with the demise of the Hon. W. H. Bruce Ogilvy. In the old line, Edward Bruce, married Anne, the sister of Robert, last pre-Reformation Bishop of Orkney and an early Lord President of the Scottish Court of Session, or Law Court. Edward and Anne were the great-grandparents of Sir William Bruce of Kinross and they lived at Blairhall, an estate about two miles due north of Culross, in Fife, where the Earl of Elgin and Kincardine, current head of the family of Bruce of Clackmannan has his principal Seat.

Robert Bruce of Blairhall, Sir William's grandfather, married Margaret, daughter of John Hamilton, the notorious last papist Archbishop of St. Andrews, who was hung at the Mercat Cross at Stirling in 1571 for taking part in an armed rebellion against the state. Their eldest son Robert, William Bruce's father, was the husband of Katherine, daughter of Sir John Preston of Valleyfield, a neighbour. Both Blairhall and Valleyfield remain on the map to this day, though neither house is of any great antiquity, while the little town of Culross, really a Royal Burgh despite its diminutive size and relative unimportance in the modern world, has recently had its interesting and evocative face lifted, to become one of the best preserved and most attractive of all the small red-tiled, white-washed Jacobean burghs in this part of Scotland. The district is still very much 'Bruce

1

country,' with the Earl of Elgin's mansion standing high above the town, overlooking the Firth of Forth. He is directly descended from Robert Bruce of Blairhall and Margaret Hamilton through their third son, Sir George Bruce, member of Parliament for Culross in the reign of James the First of England, Sixth of Scotland. The King knighted Sir George for his prowess in inventing drainage machinery whereby rich coal seams under the Forth could be worked in safety; and the new knight actually welcomed the sovereign in his own house at Culross, later escorting him down a mine, and bringing him up again on an island 'in the middle of the sea.'

Today a remarkably large proportion of the Culross which Sir George Bruce knew survives, including the crow-stepped, red-pantiled 'palas' he lived in and family tombs in the Parish Church (once attached to an ancient monastery and reputedly founded by Saint Kentigern, or Mungo, in the seventh century). Narrow cobbled streets climb inconsequentially up from the shore towards the Kirk and the Laird's house, past the saintly Bishop Leighton of Dunblane's lodging (he was a contemporary of Sir William Bruce of Kinross and tried, unsuccessfully, to reconcile episcopalian and presbyterian factions in the Scotland of Charles II), past the good bishop's turreted 'study' and on towards Blairhall and Dunfermline. Much of this was familiar to the boy William Bruce, except for the somewhat odd view southwards over the Firth of Forth, which, deriving ultimately from the pattern of industry first introduced by the Monks of Culross Abbey, and developed by their secular successor, Sir George Bruce, now reveals a smoky, unsympathetic vision of cranes and docks and oil refineries.

Dunfermline, esrtwhile capital of Scotland, and the largest town in West Fife, is quite near Blairhall on its landward side. It became the capital in the eleventh century when Malcolm Canmore moved there from Fortrenn (the modern Forteviot) in Perthshire. Malcolm married the Saxon Princess Margaret, fugitive with her brother Edgar Athelung from the Normans and descended from Alfred the Great and the early Kings of Wessex. She brought with her 'western,' or Roman Christianity, the rites and ethics of which she imposed upon the Scottish people in place of the, admittedly, irregular and occasionally heretical practices and teachings of the old Irish, or 'eastern' Church. Queen Margaret converted her husband to the Faith and she has gone down in history as a Saint. She was undoubtedly pious, though not always wise, and her bones lay, until removed to France, in the Abbey at Dunfermline which she founded. In the same place the body of King Robert the Bruce was interred in 1330. When his tomb was opened for verification in the nineteenth century the royal remains were still *in situ*, notwithstanding the destruction of the original superstructure by iconoclast Reformers.

In the lifetime of William Bruce's parents the future Charles I, last of the Royal Stewarts to be born north of the border, first saw the light of day in Dunfermline Palace, next to the ruined Abbey Church. This was the birthplace too of his sister Elizabeth of Bohemia, the 'Winter Queen,' ancestress and foundress of the present Royal House. Their mother, Anne of Denmark, spouse of King James the first of Great Britain, enjoyed the regalities of Dunfermline as part of her dowry, and it was she who restored the nave of the Abbey Church and rebuilt the adjacent palace after its bad knocking about by Knox's 'rascally mob.' She employed William Schaw, her chamberlain, to do the work, sending him to Denmark, as she later did Inigo Jones, to the Court of her brother, Christian IV, to study recent Renaissance embellishments at Elsinore Castle. Schaw designed the handsome west tower of the restored kirk, with its characteristic conical cap and battlements, which features were well known to William Bruce. In fact, Schaw's tower must have been newly finished when Bruce was yet a lad, and a common sight to him whenever he visted Pitfirrane Castle, home of Mary Halket, his bride-to-be, only two miles distant.

Pitfirrane, though belonging now to the Dunfermline Golf Club, was, until a decade or so ago, still in the hands of the Halket family who built it. The Castle covers three periods, beginning in the fifteenth century with a fortified core, and continuing to the sixteenth, with a typical laird's tower, tall, with turrets, sloping dormers and amusing heraldry. In Bruce's time the place was extended again, and thus it has remained except for a few Victorian irrelevancies. The very fine heraldry includes the Royal Arms of Scotland and the Arms of the Halkets, a shield with mantled helm 'affronty,' and for crest a falcon's head 'erased'. The supporters are two falcons, the Coat bearing 'three piles conjoined in point, on a chief a lion passant.' Beneath is the motto FIDES SUFICIT. Many years afterwards Sir William Bruce was to have these arms carved and quartered with his own 'saltire and chief, waved,' and placed, under the Bruce crest of a setting sun, over the main entrance to Kinross. They were displayed on the gateposts at the end of the long drive, his arms held by one lion, his wife's by another. The gateposts have gone, but the two lions, rescued from oblivion by the late Sir Basil Montgomery, now sit with their respective shields atop the garden wall on either side of the 'Fish Gate' overlooking Loch Leven.

William Bruce was born into a Scotland in which law and order was on the verge of breaking down. Under James VI people and King had muddled along, they understood each other and their legitimate spheres had been fairly clearly marked. Only occasionally, as when the minsiters of the kirk attempted to abrogate to themselves secular as well as spiritual powers, did trouble arise. 'The Wisest Fool in Christendom' told them to shut up. He relieved the worst offenders of their offices, set bishops over them, and appointed a Lord High Commissioner to stand between him and the clergy.

Charles I was unable to control his northern subjects as his father had done, his principles may have been higher, his motives better, but he had not been brought up in Scotland. He did not understand her curiously barbaric yet practical ways, and he liked everything cut and dried, not deliberately muddled and confused as it had been in the past. He failed in the task of governing such wayward and self-willed people, the same who eventually treated with Cromwell and executed the great Marquis of Montrose. Like the Jews, the Scots repented too late and were forced to endure a tyranny the severity of which none could have foreseen. The kind of peace, born of fear and impotence experienced in the twentieth century under Communism and Fascism, descended upon Scotland and lasted for ten years. It was this false peace, this period of puritan bigotry coupled with military control that William Bruce, then under thirty years of age, set about to end in 1658 when he made it his business to get to know General Monk, Cromwell's second-in-command, and the virtual ruler of North Britain.

The precise cause of Bruce's action, apart of course from his dislike of the régime, seems never to have been fully explained. He came, we know, of a strongly loyalist family, episcopalian and patrician, with royal blood to boot, but it must have taken some imagination and bravado, plus a perfect sense of occasion, to beard the wily Monk at his headquarters near Edinburgh, and so to persist in his purpose as to win the General's confidence and have himself sent to the King in Holland as secret envoy. Bruce is generally supposed to have pointed out to the stern, fifty-year-old Roundhead the benefits that would accrue to the man who relieved the people of their anxieties and hastened the return of the Royal Family and a normal existence. That he achieved this aim suggests that he was more than uncommonly gifted with intelligence and what was then called 'address.' The Bruce of Arnot papers speak of him as 'finding means of obtaining an interview with General Monk, and representing to him in such a striking manner the distracted state of the kingdom, and the honour that would be acquired by the man who should be instrumental in restoring the rightful heir to the throne, that the General made a confidant of the young Scot.'

The Arnot papers, some of the most intriguing of which were discovered in an Edinburgh lawyer's office when clearing up the affairs of the last direct representative of that branch of the Bruce family, are in the Register House. One feels that they may not all be contemporary with the events they describe, but even so there can be no disputing the authenticity of Sir William Bruce's passport, which descended through his only daughter Anne, and her eventual heirs, to the late Thomas Bruce Esq. of Arnot. It is made out as follows :

> 'Permitt the Bearer hereof, Mr. William Bruce, with his servant, Horses (nott exceeding the value in the proclamation), and necessaries to passe about his occasions on this side of the ffryth and other parts of Scotland and to Repasse without molestation. Hee doing nothing prejudiciall to the Commonwealth of England. Given under my hand and Seale att Dalkeith, the 7th day of September 1659.
>
> You are to permitt him to keepe his sword in his lodging till he Returns into Holland.
>
> (signed), George Monk.'

Dalkeith Palace is about five miles south of Edinburgh, on the opposite side of the Firth of Forth from where William Bruce resided, hence no doubt the permission to pass 'on this side of the ffryth' contained in the Passport. The future architect to Charles II and Clerk to the Bills must have crossed and re-crossed the Firth a good deal between the time of Cromwell's death, in 1658, and his being sent to Holland a year later by General Monk. It would be interesting to know from which port he sailed. It was probably Leith, and to Rotterdam, that was the usual route, the route by which, after the Restoration, the *objets d'art*, chimneypieces, busts and urns were brought from the Continent for Lord Lauderdale and for Bruce himself. He probably travelled from Fife to the Lothians via the Queensferry (inaugurated by Queen Margaret eight hundred years ago and only discontinued in the autumn of 1964, when H.M. Queen Elizabeth opened the new Forth Road Bridge). Certainly, some of the hazards of using the ferry in the olden days would have been reduced by Cromwell's forced pacification of the country, for the ferrymen were notoriously unreliable and extortionate. Both King James and Anne of Denmark had to take disciplinary action against them for attacking passengers, pick-pocketing, getting drunk and overcharging. They also worked on the Sabbath (no doubt at double, or treble, pay), which was expressly forbidden. The Commonwealth Government did restore some semblance of law and order, and whether one approved or not (and Bruce and his friends clearly did not), the puritan decade in Scotland was the quiestest of the whole seventeenth century. Even the usually irrepressible General Assembly was silenced. In fact it is little short of a miracle that Bruce, unknown and by no means a supporter of the régime, should have been sent abroad to parley with the exiled King.

Perhaps as curious as the circumstances of the youthful William Bruce's mission to Holland is the way in which most history books and general literature of the period bypass the incident. With so many issues at stake, so many irons in the fire, so many comings and goings it is odd that the man who set the ball rolling in the secret negotiations for the restoration of the monarchy receives no mention at all in the average text book, either for his work behind the scenes between 1658 and 1660, or as an active politician and King's Architect afterwards.

Without Monk nothing could have been achieved : he commanded the Army, an efficient and well trained force, the successor to Oliver Cromwell's 'Model Army;' and that army's march, under Monk's orders, from Coldstream to London, turned the scales in favour of Charles II. Yet Monk had to be won over first, converted from republican and puritan leanings and allegiances to monarchial and episcopalian ones. Mr William Bruce of Arnot, later of Balcaskie and subsequently of Kinross, whose age was exactly that of the King he and his friends wished to see restored to the throne, set himself the task of tackling the General and bringing him to his way of thinking. He seems to have accomplished his mission with aplomb then retired from the scene to let the seeds he had sown flourish. The former House at Dalkeith in which Cromwell's Governor of Scotland was installed is now incorporated, though not obliterated, within Dalkeith Palace, which was built towards the end of the seventeenth century (not by Bruce but by one of his principal pupils, James Smith) for Anne, Duchess of Monmouth (Duchess of Buccleuch in her own right) who retired here following the execution of her husband in 1685. There remains, however, Monk's Avenue, a line of trees planted by the General, who spent much of his time improving the Dalkeith estate, devoting himself especially to forestry and horti-culture. One can imagine him strolling up and down the newly planted avenues in earnest conversation with the young man from Fife who was so keen to see the King 'enjoy his own again.' It is our first real picture, at least mine, of Bruce in action, and one which can easily be visualised today if one visits Dalkeith.

It is when one tries to trace Bruce's earliest essay in the archi-tectural field that it is well nigh impossible to get to the root of things. It has been said, for instance, that he designed the steeple of the old Merchant's Hospital in Glasgow, the Bridgegate Steeple as it is called, but this, surely, is an untenable theory, unless the date inscribed on that structure, 1651, is incorrect. Bruce did design the steeple of the Town House at Stirling many years later, in 1703, and the master builder, Tobias Bauchop of Alloa, cribbed the details when he came to build the Mid-steeple at Dumfries; but all this is well known and the respective Burgh Records duly describe the operations. Not so with the Glasgow Steeple, for neither the City architect's department nor the City Librarian have been able to discover a single contemporary reference to Sir William Bruce's supposed connection with the Old Merchant's Hospital. Glasgow is the largest city in Scotland, with a long and honourable history, and it seems impossible that such a place should possess absolutely no record of any kind to substantiate latter day notions that Bruce worked on the Merchant's Steeple, if in fact he did. Indeed, the first statement hinting that the building was designed by him appears in James Cleland's *Annals of Glasgow*, published in 1816. 'Later writers have thought the attribution doubtful' — I quote from a letter I received from the Glasgow City Librarian. The Steeple in question is a very tall and handsome edifice in which old-fashioned Gothic and undigested early Renaissance motifs are topped by a baroque, Dutch-style cupola, and it is this last feature which may have been added by Bruce, possibly when the structure was repaired in 1659. In 1651 he was barely an adult and had certainly not yet been on his travels to the Continent. In 1659 he had been abroad once or twice for Monk, and could easily have seen a steeple similar to the one here in Glasgow.[1]

Brief mention of the Bridgegate Steeple is made in the first of four articles printed in the 'Quarterly' of the Royal Incorporation of Architects in Scotland in 1924/25. They were the work of Mr H. F. Kerr and represent, so far as is known, the only attempt since David Marshall's in 1881 to assemble in one essay a list of Sir William Bruce of Kinross's architectural achievements and record the main details of his life. Mr Kerr, rightly in my opinion, dismisses the Glasgow Steeple as a case of unproven so far as the Bruce connection is concerned. More positively he refers to the part played by the Clerk to the Bills in helping the seventh Earl of Eglinton in setting up 'manufacturies at the Citadaill of Air.' Whether or not one could classify this as a purely architectural enterprise or merely as an early example of post-war restitution and rehabilitation is a matter for conjecture, for the Citadel at Ayr had been built at great expense by Monk, on Cromwell's Orders, between the years 1654 and 1655. The project was so costly that the Protector himself was provoked into commenting that it might just as well have been built of gold! The Citadel covered more than twelve acres right in the middle of the town. Indeed it both included and encompassed old Ayr, taking in the medieval Kirk of St. John the Baptist, the tower of which survives, rising from the midst of the remains of Monk's vast fort.

It would, of course, be tempting to indulge in further speculation and suggest that Bruce may have been engaged in some previous capacity here under Monk, may have met the General during the construction of Ayr Citadel, or even the Citadel at Leith, which like the one at Ayr was dismantled and converted to civilian use at the Restoration. It was in the Citadel at Leith, curiously enough, that the second Lady Bruce, Sir William's widow, lived and set up her Jacobite cell, one of the most notorious in Scotland and frequently cited in contemporary chronicles. Nearly all well known Jacobites were taken there at one time or another. It was also from this comparatively unfashionable hideout that she sent comfort and sewing materials out to the man-of-war on which Miss Flora MacDonald was. Robert Chambers' *History of the Rebellion of 1745–6*, states that several persons made the heroine valuable presents, and 'care was taken by the widow of Sir William Bruce to send her a thimble, needles, white thread of different sorts, with some linen and cambric, cut and shaped according to the newest fashions. This piece of friendship Miss Flora admired as much as any instance of kindness and regard that had been shewn her, because all the time she had been in custody she was quite idle, having no work to do, and thereby time passed dully on.'

Lady Bruce died in 1752, almost exactly a hundred years after work began on the Cromwellian Citadel she was to inhabit for so long.[2] Did her future husband have a hand in the building? It would be fascinating to know. Could he possibly have begun his architectural career in the service of the Commonwealth in his twenties? It would certainly explain how he found it possible on Cromwell's demise to win the confidence of Monk with so little effort, for it was Monk who, on behalf of Cromwell, superintended the construction of both Leith and Ayr Citadels. It is not an unreasonable supposition either, for Bruce's cousin, Eliza Murray, daughter of Catherine Bruce of Clackmannan and William Murray (subsequently first Earl of Dysart), became the confidante, and it is said, mistress of the Lord Protector, as a rhyming lampoon of the period declares.

'She is Besse of my heart, she was Besse of Old Noll.'

Eliza's husband, Sir Lionel Tollemache, had been the whipping-boy for Charles I, being physically punished for his young master's mild misdemeanours; but she did not find him nearly ambitious enough for her taste. She meant to reach the heights and manipulate the male wielders of fate, so she turned her charm onto ugly, warted Oliver, and seems to have bent him to her will. She also assessed the future with considerable cunning, deciding, long in advance, that the King would eventually be restored to his own again and that if she played her cards right she would have a big part to play in that event as well. Accordingly, having chosen a second husband while her first was still alive, she obtained the release, through her ascendancy over Cromwell, of the Earl, later Duke, of Lauderdale, Charles II's Commissioner to-be in Scotland and a member of the infamous Restoration *Cabal*. She acquired the title of Countess of Dysart in her father's right, and when Sir Lionel Tollemache died she married Lauderdale, six weeks after his Countess's death!

One wonders, therefore, if William Bruce, who was later to obtain large and important commissions through his scheming cousin Eliza, often visited her at Ham in the days of Cromwell, and was perhaps taken to see Coleshill, in Berkshire, the last and best of the 'Inigo Jones' country houses. It was completed, probably by Sir Roger Pratt, about 1652. Was he also a visitor to Thorpe Hall, near Peterborough, another of the better known Palladian exercises, this time by Jones's nephew, John Webb, and Ashburnham House, London? These three 'classical' essays undoubtedly became familiar to him at some time or another, though whether it was before or after the Restoration is difficult to assess. His own wonderful house at Kinross, which he began in 1689, is said, erroneously, or only as a half-truth, to be a copy of Coleshill. Though the sight of the English model may have had some bearing on Bruce's thought he certainly did not copy it as anyone can see by comparing drawings and plans. Nor does Kinross resemble Thorpe Hall much more than Coleshill, though there are a few similar internal features. The staircase at Ashburnham on the other hand, almost certainly designed by Inigo Jones himself, has a decided reflection in the style and taste of the entrance hall at Kinross. The original is in the purest Italian manner, without a trace of baroque, and Bruce seems to have remembered it long afterwards. In the end, however, Ham was probably the English House he knew best and from which he gleaned interesting ideas. He even designed the gates there for his patroness-cousin, the powerful Countess of Dysart. Indeed, it was after completing this small commission to her satisfaction that he was entrusted with grander, more exclusive contracts, for herself and the Duke of Lauderdale, and this led to his being appointed Surveyor to the King in Scotland.

It is a far cry from the splendours of Ham to the setting up of factories at Ayr on the site of a Cromwellian fort, but one has to begin somewhere, and Bruce's interest and part in providing work and homes for the unemployed of Ayr is typical of him, if untypical of the age. Besides holding the office of Clerk to the Bills, in 1665 he was made Clerk of Supply to the Lords in Council to collect sums imposed on persons bringing actions into the Scottish Court of Session and normally payable to the King. In 1667 he was given the post of Collector of Taxes imposed by Act of Parliament for payment of the Forces, and in the same year was appointed Superintendent and

Overseer of the Palaces of Holyroodhouse, Stirling, Edinburgh Castle, The Bass Rock, Dumbarton Castle, Falkland Palace etc., 'within the Kingdoms of Scotland, France and Ireland.' His Baronetcy came in 1668. In 1671 he was put in charge of the rebuilding of Holyroodhouse for the King, with the title of Surveyor-General of H.M. the King's Works in Scotland (the complementary office to that held by Sir Christopher Wren in England). Ten years later Bruce was enrolled (at Royal suggestion) as Commissioner for the Shire of Kinross, and this date, 1681, probably marks the summit of a political life which, on the face of it, looks as conformist and place-seeking as any other in Restoration times.[3]

His rise was rapid, to say the least, and was not just due to services rendered to the King in exile but to the influence of wealthy and interested relations and friends, the Countess of Dysart principally, her Murray relations, the Dukes of Lauderdale and Rothes (Bruce's son John married Rothes' daughter), the Hopes of Craighall (Anne Bruce married Sir Thomas Hope of Craighall), and a host of other cross relationships either marital or political. Yet, and this is the whole point about Bruce, as public servant and architect he displayed a sense of purpose compartively rare in his day and which was, when his patrons and friends were removed, to bring him into trouble with new masters, when 'a stranger filled the Stewart throne.' He had helped to engineer the return of Charles II and the re-establishment of episcopacy. For a quarter of a century afterwards he was on the winning side. It is as simple as that. He reaped what he had sown; but when the Stewarts were deposed and a presbyterian form of church government established he did not change his coat as so many others did or tried to do, but he remained faithful to his beliefs and suffered for them for the rest of his long life.

It has been said by the ignorant that he found the money to build Kinross House by unjustly penalising the Covenanters, but the records do not confirm this, in fact, they suggest the very opposite. Bruce took no advantage of his position as Sheriff to extract excessive punishments or fines, nor to divert the taxes he collected for the supply of the Army to private ends.[4] Old 'Besse' was another matter, she and Lauderdale were by no means above reproach, indeed Lauderdale had Bruce dismissed from his post as Surveyor to the King before Holyrood was finished and caused his brother, Lord Hatton, to be appointed instead, though Hatton was no architect, only a lawyer. Rothes was eclipsed by men more ruthless, and by 1685, when Bruce moved to the Loch Leven estate on which Kinross is sited, he had already begun to shed his public duties and devote more and more time to the practice of architecture and landscape gardening. His work at the Citadel of Ayr therefore marks a real beginning of his professed career, and it was done in the same year as he bought Balcaskie, that Laird's tower in Fife which he was to make his workshop. It was the place where he experimented both as architect and gardener, the power-house from which he was to draw the experience necessary to make him the principal architect of the Kingdom, which he remained until his death, at the age of eighty, in 1710.

1 R. G. Cant and I. G. Lindsay, in their *Old Glasgow*, published in 1947, say; 'The design (of the Merchant's House Steeple), which is attributed on very doubtful authority to Sir Wm. Bruce, is a delightful compound of Gothic and Renaissance features.'

2 In 1761 there was advertised for sale 'the commodious dwelling house . . . possessed by Lady Bruce . . . having 13 fire rooms, stables and chaise-house.'

3 About this time Sir William entered into a bond with the Earl of Haddington and others to commission the Privateer 'Bruce,' which in 1683 captured the foreign ships 'Patience' and 'Palmetrie.' He was sent to London by his companions to claim the 'Prize Money' and arrange a just division a year later.

4 A typical document from his term as Sheriff at Kinross is the Warrant, dated May 23rd, 1682, to James Dempster and his spouse 'to brew and sell ale and beer, tobacco, candles and spices.'

Chateau de Blerancourt, arch and pavilions

CHAPTER TWO

Balcaskie to Holyroodhouse

WILLIAM BRUCE bought Balcaskie in 1665 from Sir John Moncreiffe of that Ilk, who then not only sold his own family seat at Moncreiffe to his cousin Thomas, but relinquished his hereditary rights to the same cousin, who thus became Sir Thomas of that Ilk. Sir John then retired into undisturbed bachelordom. The link between Bruce and the Moncreiffes had begun earlier, for Sir Thomas had served with Bruce on the 'Secret but Royal Committee' formed to visit Charles II in exile in Holland, and like Bruce he had been rewarded at the Restoration with a government post, in his case that of Clerk to the Exchequer. There was another Moncreiffe link through the retiring Sir John, whose mother was Lady Mary Murray (daughter of the second Earl of Tullibardine and sister of the first Earl of Atholl) which led to Bruce obtaining the commission to rebuild Dunkeld House, the Earl of Atholl's seat, ruined by fighting between Cromwellians and royalists in 1654. The restoration of Dunkeld may have been the young architect's first full-scale job: at any rate the late Duke of Atholl is reported as holding that view.

Balcaskie was Bruce's workshop as well as his first country house, and the property from which he took his title, until he bought the Loch Leven estate and built Kinross. At Balcaskie, which has survived virtually intact, one can see his early experiments in formal planning, his introduction into Scotland of the contemporary classical mode. Besides his secret journeyings on the Continent in the last years of the Cromwellian dictatorship, Bruce made an extensive trip to France in 1663, which is mentioned by Lauderdale in one of his letters, written in 1671 in thanks for a later expedition made on his behalf to Holland in search of *articles de vertu*, 'floral' stone and valuable timbers. A Bill of Lading also confirms such commissions, one referring to building materials shipped by William Wallace, 'Marchand in Edinburgh,' on the 'Anna off Pyttinweams,' with John Atchison Master, the goods coming from Rotterdam. Pittenweem is the nearest small town, and port, to Balcaskie, and it is clear that besides transporting marble, 'trees', vases and 'plamoy' for the King's Commissioner, and for the Earl, later Duke, of Rothes (a near neighbour in Fife) Bruce brought quite a lot over for himself to use in the beautiful 'Italian' terracing at Balcaskie; and for the embellishment of the niches in the curving wing walls he built on either side of the main entrance to the house. These niches now contain urns, but they almost certainly once contained the busts of Roman Emperors since removed to the garden.

The wing wall idea he may have seen at Ham House. The niches there are provided with a mixture of Roman Emperors and contemporary figures (I seem to remember the busts of Charles I and Charles II somewhere); but I do not think Bruce copied Ham in this particular, for it was not until after 1673 that Ham House as we know it was created out of an older, Jacobean residence, and Bruce probably introduced wing walls into the North himself. It was surely no mere accident either that the greatest hemicycled forecourt in Christendom, Bernini's colonnaded Piazza San Pietro in Rome, was abuilding between the years 1656 and 1667. This sensational achievement for its day (it can still amaze the beholder) must have been tremendous, and Bruce would not have needed to go to Italy in order to appreciate it. I have found nothing in the records to show that he ever did cross the Alps, and the standard of the 'Italian' statuary and other details at Balcaskie is not really high enough to warrant their having come direct from the land of Michelangelo.

It is undeniable, however, that William Bruce could have met 'Il Cavaliere Bernini' in the flesh, in Paris, on one of his post-Restoration trips on the Contiennt, for shortly after completing St. Peter's Square the Italian 'maestro' was invited to France to submit drawings for a new Louvre (his scheme was so thorough that it included the demolition of all existing portions of that historic building, and he was eventually sent home, politely but firmly, without getting the job). Bernini's design for the eastern façade of the Louvre (discarded in favour of one by Perrault) was described by one of the adjudicators for the competition as 'fenestrated sculpture,' and not without some justification since its extreme *Italianita* flew violently in the face of Gallic logic and restraint. It was this same logic and restraint, incidentally, that Bruce admired so and which marks him out as entirely different from many of his English contemporaries. I exclude Wren, for he, perhaps alone in Restoration England, was not interested in decoration for decoration's sake; though he did go to Paris in the hopes of catching a glimpse of Bernini's design for the Louvre, and seems to have managed, if not to study the drawings, at least to have had a word with their creator before he returned home.

An earlier example of the formal use of curved wing walls to create an architectural mood and draw the beholder in, almost to embrace him as he approaches the building, occurred in Palladio's scheme for the Villa Trissina, near Venice, and which undoubtedly inspired Paine's plan for Kedleston, in Derbyshire, completed a century later than Sir William Bruce's work at Balcaskie. According to Mr Kerr (in the R.I.A.S. 'Quarterly') Bruce actually tried out the winged entrance first at Panmure, in Forfarshire, but there is no means of checking this since the drawings do not indicate any obvious winged walls, and photographs taken shortly before it was blown up by dynamite, in 1955, show it much enlarged and altered, and hardly a Bruce house at all. One thing is clear, however — Bruce had a strong penchant for the hemicycle, and he did not get it from any French example as there were none to be seen when he visited France in his young days; he may have got it from drawings of Trissina, or from the Bernini's *chef d'œuvre* in Rome, or even from some little known example by Jones, but in any event he made it fashionable. More than that, he made it practical as well. To Bruce an architectural feature was no mere ornament, it had to have some practical use as well as look good, and the curved entrance wings he built, concave at Balcaskie, Harden (Mertoun) and Auchendinny, convex at Kinross and Hopetoun (the latter afterwards being rebuilt the opposite way by William Adam) had a function to perform : they screened corridors and servants' quarters, gardeners' tool stores, back yards, all sorts of things which interested neither Bernini nor Palladio. To the theatrical Italians architecture was stage scenery, man was made for it, not the other way round. Bruce believed that architecture was made for man, and we shall find this borne out over and over again as we trace his career in the 'Mistress Art.'

What did Bruce see in France in 1663 ? Well, he must undoubtedly have made himself acquainted with the accepted architectural masterpieces of the day : not Versailles, as it had not been built, but Vaux-le-Vicomte, the splendid landscaping of which was soon to be reflected in Bruce's own grand vistas. The one at Balcaskie, for instance, stretches out for miles from his "Italian" terraces, through contrived clearances in the woods, to reveal, far on the other side of the Firth of Forth, the majestic Bass Rock. Again, at Kinross, where the house is sited axially and equi-distant from its monumental gates (in the town), and Loch Leven Castle (on an island in the loch of the same name), the formal layout is on a prodigious scale. At Hopetoun, Auchendinny and Mertoun intelligent use of existing landmarks, plus complementary statuary, framing avenues and immense platforms of grass and gravel, also demonstrate the architect's understanding and appreciation of gardening and planning *a la francaise*.

1　General Monk, Duke of
Albemarle. School of Lely

2　King Charles II by John
Michael Wright

3 Parish Church at Balleroy, Normandy, by François Mansart

4 Chateau de Balleroy built by François Mansart before 1630

5   Manoir de Brécy, Normandy. Designed as a
wedding present for his niece, Renée Le Bas, by
F. Mansart

6   Vista and Ercole de Farnese at Vaux-le-Vicomte
(1656–61). Le Nôtre

7 Eliza Murray, Countess
of Dysart, afterwards
Duchess of Lauderdale.
Portrait at Ham by Sir
Peter Lely

8 The Duke of Lauderdale.
Portrait painted by Lely for
the Duke of Rothes and
formerly at Leslie House

The true Renaissance had been introduced into France in the sixteenth century, first by Florentines brought in by François Premier and later by Catherine de Médicis (Queen of Henri II), but apart from the expert and tasteful work of Phillibert de l'Orme, French architecture, no longer directed by trained Italian 'masters,' subsequently deteriorated into an ill-digested *melange* of crude Florentine-inspired ornament applied to the remnants of overblown native Gothic. This, of course, is exactly what happened in Britain as well until Inigo Jones arrived on the scene in the south and Sir William Bruce in the north. Across the Channel taste began to revive under the patronage of Marie de Médicis (consort of Henri IV, mother of Henrietta Maria and grandmother of the 'Merry Monarch'). Not much enamoured of her husband, whose mistresses were legion (and whose religion was suspect), the pious Marie pined for Tuscany and the graces of her native Florence, its architecture in particular. She employed Salomon de Brosse to design the Luxembourg Palace in the style of the Palazzo Pitti and was responsible for the erection in the Luxembourg Gardens of that most effusive of Italianate French fountains, the Fontaine de Médicis, in which De Brosse introduced into northern Europe the *bossage* and *congelations* of the south, the rustications, vegetation and 'freezings' of an over sophisticated society in search of 'barbaric' diversions. Bruce adopted the icicles and *bossage* for the decoration of his 'Fish Gate' at Kinross, facing the loch. This was about the year 1685, and the closest contemporary specimens elsewhere in Britain are the frost-work grotto and cascade temple at Chatsworth, which are dated about 1690 and have a more pronounced Italian source — probably Papal Roman.

William Bruce was acquainted, one feels sure, with the Château de Blérancourt, north of Paris, with its ambitious garden architecture and formal layout, again by De Brosse. The Château, completed before 1620, is now much altered and has become a museum to Franco-American co-operation in the 1914–18 War, though its gazebos, triumphal arches and *parterres* remain and can be seen to have affected the Scottish architect's work both at Kinross and Balcaskie. Perhaps Bruce was even more influenced by the buildings and garden plans of François Mansart, great-uncle of the better known Jules-Hardouin (who began Versailles for 'le Roi Soleil'). A minor masterpiece of Mansart's was and is the Château de Balleroy, in Normandy. It was the first serious attempt to use classical Renaissance ideas of symmetry and ornament in a genuinely French setting, indeed, unlike, say, Inigo Jones, who introduced the Palladian mode direct and undiluted from Venice, Mansart, more in the spirit of William Bruce in Scotland a generation later, tamed Italian theatricality to Gallic tastes and the result is a chaste and ordered style of building with refined decoration which has scarcely been excelled.

Balleroy, which is seen and approached via a very long straight avenue, is a typical exercise in which reason and good taste join to make a harmonious and well — nigh perfect whole, a thing sufficient in itself and not amenable to alteration or enlargement. The long straight avenue, first of village houses, then of trees and finally of estate outhouses, leads to a platform punctuated by corner pavilions and ornamental *poivrettes* (a concession to lingering Gothic traditions). Regularised paths and steps bring one to the front door. The building materials used are pleasantly varied, with fine Caen stone for quoins and surrounds and a blackish local schist for infilling. The roof is *a la francaise*, that is tall and nearly pointed, and at the centre rises a fine cupola. Inside are the furnishings of the Louis XIII period, bolection mouldings, richly painted plaster ceilings, baroque panellings, and a handsome stone staircase. In short, Balleroy is a sort of French Ham House, with so much of 'Bruce' in it one feels almost certain he must have been there and examined the place thoroughly, indeed, improved on it in some respects. There are no curving wing walls here, only stiff rectangular links between corner pavilions and house; and Mansart was not nearly so clever with his chimneys as Bruce, who always disposed them on inner walls, which helped to keep the house warm inside and to create a good upstanding architectural appearance outside. Chimneys, of course, were one of Bruce's *fortes*. — yet another sign of his highly developed practical sense.

At the gates to Balleroy stands the Parish Church, generally assumed to have been the work of Mansart at the same time as the château. It is a plainish cruciform structure with a central tower capped by a simple octagonal roof. It reminds one very much of Lauder Kirk, in Berwickshire, which Bruce designed for the Duke of Lauderdale in 1673, when he was busy on Thirlestane Castle near by. Nor is Mansart's example confined to these two noble designs at Balleroy, for at Brécy, on the eastern side of Bayeux, still in Normandy, is the Manoir de Brécy, the plans for which Mansart gave as a present to his niece, Renée Le Bas, on her marriage. The house is as near the scale of Auchendinny as makes no matter, a shade grander, and the garden, which is the *bout du voyage* of Brécy, rises behind in terraces in the purest "Italian" manner. If Bruce did not see Brécy then all I can say is he must have dreamt he did. The Manoir is approached through a small courtyard, squarish, and screened from the road by a surprisingly elaborate gateway, almost a triumphal arch, with lions on either side holding the shield of the Le Bas family. Similar lions, only cleverly devised with two faces, turned in different directions, are in the garden. They are remarkably like the two stone lions at Kinross, on either side of the 'Fish Gate.'

At Balcaskie Bruce busied himself over a number of years, from the day he bought it, in 1665, to the day he sold it, to Sir Thomas Stewart of Grantully, in 1684/5. The Terraces he constructed *de novo*, much on the lines of Brécy; and the celebrated vista towards the Bass Rock we can trace fairly easily to ideas gleaned at Vaux-le-Vicomte. As for the house proper, it is, as I have already indicated, not so much a novelty as an experimental workshop wherein the architect-laird tried out his brain-waves before launching forth on grander, more ambitious ploys. Roughly speaking Sir William Bruce applied himself to two main types of building (that is, of houses). Balcaskie was of the first, and in some ways most typical, in that, as at Holyrood, an existing structure was adapted rather than replaced, its main features repeated; the duplicated and original parts then being joined by a new linking element, thus making a symmetrical whole. Brunstane and Thirlestane, both renovated and enlarged for the Duke of Lauderdale, are further examples of this treatment. The second type, of course, was a brand new building in the classical idiom, either on a virgin site or on the ruins of something that had gone before. Dunkeld and Moncreiffe Houses are good early examples of complete re-buildings on old sites. Bruce had a high regard for historical precedent, and did not despise past styles of architecture as the Georgians were to, nor did he consider the Gothic age as necessarily barbaric. He liked above all to relate his new or restored buildings to something interesting that had gone before, and at Balcaskie this was comparatively easy. He sited it on the Bass Rock and incorporated in the design Scotch Baronial motifs, repeating dormer windows, gun loops and out-of-date water spouts; generally preparing himself for a commission that came his way in 1672, when he was asked to make Thirlestane Castle, medieval Border Seat of the Lauderdales, a suitable home for his grandest patrons.

At Balcaskie Bruce only 'played' with Baronial features, but did not make a fetish of them. Indeed, the northern façade of the house is as formal and French as it could be, approached as it is by curving wings and two pavilions whose spareness and nobly proportioned severity is only relieved by ashlar quoins and margins, and softened by hipped roofs. It may be worth mentioning that these pavilions, in which the architect showed how well he had studied French taste, and especially the art of knowing where to stop, served as models for many a later building by Bruce right up to the end of his life. One recalls, particularly, outhouses at Auchendinny and at Hopetoun, even the Hopetoun Aisle at Abercorn Kirk. The pavilions at Balcaskie are not of gazebo stature but are really small houses containing a laundry and coach house respectively; though they do not seem at all large

17

when set on either side of a vast expanse of, I was going to say, nothing, but the gravel space in front of Balcaskie is another of Bruce's calculated voids, and is exactly right for the size of the house wings and pavilions, and providing a perfect proscenium before the front door.

Inside as outside Bruce experimented in this, his own first house; and noteworthy at Balcaskie are the fretwork ceilings by George Dunsterfield, whose presence here is confirmed by extant bills and accounts (he received 3/6d Scots a day for his labours), in 1674. He and John Halbert were King Charles II's favourite ornamental plasterers, they worked at Windsor Castle in the State Apartments and came up to Scotland to do the King's Bedchamber and other rooms at Holyrood, as well as private ceilings at Thirlestane, and here in Fife. Dunsterfield also went on to make the lovely fretwork ceiling over the stairs at Kinross. The main characteristic of these elaborate creations is their depth of relief and the extreme realism achieved thereby. They usually revolved around a central wreath composed of fruit and flowers, and in origin they seem to have derived, pretty directly, from the rich *trompe l'œil* ceiling by Andrea Mantegna in the *Sala degli Sposi* of the ducal Palace at Mantua (even down to the odd birds perched on the edge of the floral wreath which frames the central panel). These birds, a cross between eagles and vultures, actually recur on one of the Caroline ceilings at Kellie Castle, a neighbouring house to Balcaskie and the childhood home of the renowned Scottish architect, the late Sir Robert Lorimer, whose father restored the castle. The vulture-eagles also appear at Holyrood, painted by Jacob de Wett on a central panel of one of Dunsterfield and Halbert's elaborate ceilings there. De Wett was the man responsible for those quaint portraits of more than a hundred genuine and supposed royal ancestors of Charles II that line the Long Gallery of the rebuilt palace.

It is unlikely that any of the ceilings we have been talking about could have been done before 1672, and they are all probably later, which means that Bruce managed to get hold of Dunsterfield's services while or after he was engaged at Holyrood. In fact, this is really proved by the survival at Balcaskie of two charming ceilings in old fashioned Jacobean style put up in 1665/6, one coved and finished with a pendant globe at the centre, the other gay with the usual cherubs, and thistle and rose devices, and the entwined intitials of the owners, in this case W B and M H, for William Bruce and Mary Halket. They are in the old part of the house, upstairs, and make a remarkable contrast to the lush 'wigglemarees' of the three main rooms on the *piano nobile*, which would not disgrace the State Apartments at Holyrood. Dunsterfield, or his assistants, probably

18

did the Caroline ceilings at Kellie Castle whilst still busy at Balcaskie, and Bruce himself is credited with the chimneys there, circa 1676. In fact he had a lot of irons in the fire at the time, Panmure, in Forfarshire; Leslie House, in Fife; Dunkeld; and probably Moncreiffe House as well.

Letters and accounts show that Panmure was built, or at any rate begun by John Mylne, Master Mason to the King, shortly after the Restoration, and that the house stood on a site some distance away from an older castle. Bruce is generally supposed to have produced the plans, indeed this is mentioned in various documents though no drawings or plans of his exist, and those shown by William Adam in *Vitruvius Scoticus* do not give the name of the architect. Mylne died in 1667 and was succeeded as King's Mason by his nephew, Robert Mylne, who built Holyrood in the following decade under Sir William Bruce's supervision. He is not it seems connected with Panmure, which was completed by another mason. Jacob de Wett painted 'ane picture' for the third Earl of Panmure and charged him £6 Scots (10/- English money), for it; and in 1672, and again in 1693, Bruce made alterations and additions to the house, including the provision of formal gates.

John Mylne also worked at Leslie House, in Fife, where Bruce was positively in charge, and it is unfortunate that this building, which must have been both magnificent and interesting for its period, has not survived except for one much mutilated wing. It was a big house, in fact, when its owner, the Earl of Rothes, became Lord Chancellor and was made a Duke, he had it enlarged to outshine Holyrood; and the Long Gallery and other apartments were deliberately made one foot larger all round for that purpose. It was a square courtyard structure, of which one side alone remains, greatly altered, and looked rather 'Scotch' on the front but was very Palladian and formal on the court side. In 1670 Lady Rothes was engaged in sending furniture and hangings, leather and draperies, north from London to Leslie House, which was known later as Rothes Palace. A letter in the Kinross Papers lists her proposals and requirements for Bruce's benefit. John Bruce, of course, the architect's only son, married Lady Christian Leslie, daughter of the Duke and Duchess of Rothes, who had previously been married to the third Marquis of Montrose, and her son by that bond, the future first Duke of Montrose, was actually brought up in his step-father's home at Kinross. There is an odd story told that Rothes Palace was made as large and magnificent as it was not to please the Duke of Rothes but James, Duke of York, Charles II's brother, who, excluded from his position in England by the Test Act, intended to retire there when the King died. There is no proof of this and the same story has been applied to Kinross House. James was certainly 'exiled' to Scotland for three years, between 1679 and 1683, and resided in Bruce's reconstructed Palace at Holyrood; but whether he would ever have given up his right to the throne is highly problematical, and in the event he certainly did not.

It is a great pity Panmure House was demolished without a blow being struck for its retention as an historical and significant Scottish monument, and that its destruction took place suddenly and before any of the interested bodies could get moving in its defence. This sort of thing is happening every day, even though there exists ample machinery for holding up precipitous action of the kind while the 'pros and cons' are properly and quietly examined both by experts and the established authorities. The virtual destruction of Leslie House, however, could scarcely be blamed on the Philistines, since it was accidently burned down and only partially rebuilt in 1767. Moncreiffe House, in Perthshire, also perished in flames, but as recently as 1958, when the laird was burned to death in his own home, after rushing back, it is said, to save his dogs. Dunkeld was demolished by its Hanoverian owner and nothing remains but the site, a beautiful one, overlooking the ruins of Dunkeld Cathedral. It is possible that certain internal fittings at Blair, such as late Stewart panelling and ornate 'Grinling-Gibbon-type' mouldings on the stairs and adjoining rooms, may have come from the old Bruce house, when Blair Castle was converted into a classical mansion in the southern English manner.

The first Dunkeld House, a laird's tower really, was badly damaged in a running fight between Royalists and Cromwellians in 1654, and as soon as practicable after the Restoration John, second Earl of Tullibardine and first Murray Earl of Atholl, set about its rebuilding, employing William Bruce as architect. It may be remembered that the Earl's sister was the mother of that Sir John Moncreiffe who sold Balcaskie to Bruce in 1665 and Moncreiffe House itself to Sir Thomas Moncreiffe in 1667. To say precisely which came first, the restoration of Dunkeld or the building of Moncreiffe is well nigh impossible, both commissions clearly coming through the same connection, the Moncreiffes of Moncreiffe, and as a result of Bruce's purchase of Balcaskie from Sir John of that Ilk in 1665. However, I am plumping for Dunkeld first, and not just on account of the date over the main entrance at Moncreiffe (1679) but because the Slezer print of Dunkeld, which shows the new house finished, is dedicated to 'Lord James Murray, Colonel of H.M's. First Regiment of Foot Guards,' (fourth Earl of Tullibardine), who died in 1670. John Slezer, a Captain of the Artillery Company, made a reputation for himself as a recorder of the 'sights' of Scotland as they existed in the late Stewart period. Originally he simply made drawings off his own bat and offered them hopefully, as one imagines in the case of Dunkeld House, to supposedly interested persons, but later, having been made 'Surveyor of Their Majesties Stores and Magazines in the Kingdom of Scotland,' he made good use of his official travelling post to assemble a comprehensive volume of some three dozen views in his *Theatrum Scotiae*, which, in its way, served as a visual companion to Daniel Defoe's census, made at the request of Queen Anne's Government in preparation for the Union of the Scots and English Parliaments in 1707.

Slezer's *Prospect of the Town of Dunkeld* first appeared in print about 1678, and it shows, across the river, next to the Cathedral, a large squarish building with symmetrically disposed chimneys (a sure sign of Bruce), capped with a typical Restoration 'lanthorn' or cupola. At the four corners are small 'pepperpots,' indicative of the architect's habit of relating his new works to earlier ones whenever there was a chance to do so. Dunkeld House, which this handsome building undoubtedly is, could have been Sir William Bruce's very first completely original design, and although exact details are not easily discernible from the seventeenth century 'prospect' one can make out enough to see that in general principle the building was a typical Charles II mansion, all but the 'pepperpots' and the chimneys, which repeat Bruce's respect for tradition in one case and his practicality and ingenuity in the other.

Judging from faded photographs and old prints Moncreiffe House must have been the model for Kinross, the' try-out', shall we say. Like others Bruce tackled it stood on an old site, though not necessarily exactly where any previous building had been, otherwise he would have adopted the Balcaskie method and enlarged and formalised what was already there, instead of starting afresh. Moncreiffe was a brand new mansion, slightly smaller than Kinross but similar both in general feeling and in some details. It was what is called a 'double-house,' that is to say, two rooms thick, and it possessed one of those splendid wooden staircases with rich baroque carving of which the only comparable example left north of the border is now at Kinross. English models include the stairs at Thorpe Hall (a largely Cromwellian house which I have mentioned before), and Eltham Lodge, Kent, which is a royal property and was completed about 1664, by Hugh May. The link between May and Bruce could be much nearer than is usually supposed, or even guessed, for May was appointed by Charles II to do at Windsor Castle almost precisely what Bruce was appointed to do at Holyrood, to convert and enlarge an ancient and hoary 'château' into a comfortable and richly decorative home for a culturally perspicacious but indulgent monarch and his modish court.

The Dutch influence is much in evidence in Hugh May's work, more so than in Bruce's; and it was May who probably invented the small English country house which, perhaps for want of a better name, or out of sheer ignorance, is usually labelled 'Queen Anne.' He died, in 1684, when the Princess Anne of York still had twenty years to wait before becoming 'Great Anna whom three realms obey.'

Neither the staircase at Thorpe Hall nor that at Eltham Lodge can quite compare in grace and elegance with the one at Kinross, in the design of which Sir William Bruce managed to eradicate all sense of heaviness while retaining a characteristically rich and aristocratic pattern of intricate carving. Perhaps the ability of the carvers had something to do with this too, for they were Dutchmen who came specially from Holland to work for him. Some had had experience at Holyrood, where, however, there is no staircase of this kind, and indeed the only thing remotely like it, and that copied in wrought-iron, not wood, is at Caroline Park, the Edinburgh 'cottage' of Viscount Tarbet, Lord Chief Justice General of Scotland under William and Mary. This does not tell us if the staircase at Moncreiffe House was as good as the one at Kinross, but one must suppose so. One may also suppose, I think, that there were similar staircases at Dunkeld and Harden (Mertoun); but if so they no longer exist. The pictures of Moncreiffe show a fine *perron* at the entrance, about the same as Mertoun, slightly smaller than Kinross, the usual well disposed windows and strategically placed chimneys. I am quite sure there was also a cupola : Dunkeld had one, Kinross still has, and Mertoun used to have one (it is shown in the drawing in *Vitruvius Scoticus*).

The date, 1679, carved over the door at Moncreiffe House, has another significance, for it was about then that considerable tree planting was undertaken in the surrounding park, including a beech avenue 600 yards long with a small stone circle in the middle. This landscaping programme may even have taken place concurrently with operations at Kinross, where Sir William Bruce had the garden and park completed before he began work on the house itself. Trees came from London, Holland, different parts of Scotland and from France; and one cannot help feeling that some at least of the layout at Moncreiffe was part of the architect's pilot scheme for his own house and grounds. The circle in the middle sounds especially like him, and the great length of the avenue, 1800 feet, or a third of a mile, must have been without precedent in contemporary Scotland.[1] The results of these plantings are still visible, though two of the most ancient trees, a horsechestnut at Moncreiffe ($20\frac{1}{2}$ feet in girth and said to be the largest in the United Kingdom) was probably there in 1675, while a large and hoary walnut, said to be the oldest and largest of its species, at Kinross, was thought by Mr Marshall to be similarly already standing in the seventeenth century.

¹ The celebrated Beech Avenue at Melville House, in Fife, now cut down, was planted by the 1st Earl of Melville about the year 1700 either at the instigation of Bruce or his assistant, James Smith, who is thought to have completed the house about 1701.

Moncreiffe House (now rebuilt)

CHAPTER THREE

Holyrood and the Lauderdales

To say that Sir William Bruce was appointed Superintendent and Overseer of the Palaces of Holyroodhouse, Stirling, Edinburgh Castle etc., 'within the Kingdoms of Scotland, France and Ireland,' wholly through the influence of his patron the Earl, later Duke, of Lauderdale (Charles II's Secretary of State for Scotland) would be an exaggeration, for after all, 'no one in Scotland probably contributed more in a private capacity to bring about the Restoration,' to quote the *Dictionary of National Biography*, than Bruce himself. Yet he was never really in the highest counsels of State, and although Eliza Murray, Countess of Dysart and future Duchess of Lauderdale, was a cousin of his, that scheming, rapacious woman was more interested in personal power than helping far away and fairly distant relatives. She only married Lauderdale because he was as ambitious and unscrupulous as herself, and lustful for control of the King. Indeed a contemporary rhyme begins:

'Methinks this poor land has been troubled too long
With Hutton and Dysart and old Lidington,
These fools who at once make us love and despair
And preclude all the ways to his Majesty's ear.'

Hutton, really Charles Maitland (Lord Hatton) was Lauderdale's brother, and 'old Lidington' represents Lauderdale himself, Lidington, or Leithington, (since renamed Lennoxlove for reasons I will explain) being the Maitland Seat near Haddington, in East Lothian.

'She's Bessie of the Church and Bessie of the State,
She plots with her tail, and her lord with his pate,'

goes on the rhyming attack, and:

'Since the King did permit her to come to Whytehall
She outviews Cleveland, Portsmouth, young Fraser, and all.'

'Young Fraser,' the future Lady Peterborough, was one of the 'Windsor Beauties,' painted by Sir Peter Lely and now hanging in

24

Hampton Court. The artist represented Charles's 'ladies,' though they were not all his mistresses. 'La Belle Stewart' was not, and it was she who, after eloping with the Duke of Richmond and Lennox to avoid the King's attentions, subsequently made Leithington her home and renamed it so attractively, Lennoxlove.

'Besse of old Noll' was permitted to come to Whytehall largely on account of Charles II's long standing friendship with Lauderdale, a friendship formed in the days of the Civil War when the King was a mere youth; a friendship which landed Lauderdale in jail, and under sentence of death, but from which he was rescued through the good offices and prescience of Lady Dysart. At the Restoration this far-seeing act on Bessie's part bore its reward for the King made his old friend Secretary for Scotland, and he became the 'L' of the infamous CABAL that ruled Britain from behind the scenes. The lady was widowed in 1669, when her ineffectual first husband (ineffectual from her point of view) left her free to cultivate the intimate association of the most powerful man in Scotland and prime puller of strings in the Royal circle. She could not marry him straight away, he had a wife (who did not die until 1672), but she obviously had patience as well as ambition, and within weeks of Lauderdale becoming a widower he was re-wed to Eliza Murray, when the King created him a Duke!

During this time Sir William Bruce too was rising in the political and architectural world, but at home. He certainly stayed with the lady whose mother was born Catherine Bruce, and whose bust may be seen in the 'round gallery' at Ham beside a Lely portrait of 'Both ye Graces in one picture.' A letter written to Bruce by the Earl of Rothes in 1663 speaks of Lauderdale's and his arrival and reception at Court; 'My Lord Lauderdale was maid very welcome at Court: I shall not have the vanity to say so of myself: But he and I never sighted in London til we came to Whythall . . . I shall wish you a great many . . . Bills . . . etc.' The recipient had been made Clerk to the Bills as a monetary recompense for his work on the secret council which restored the King to the throne. The writer, who was Lord Chancellor of Scotland, and who had been at least as loyal as Lauderdale to the Royal House during the Civil War and Commonwealth, did not achieve the same prominence, and though being created a Duke in 1680 he neither courted nor was courted by the Countess of Dysart. His Dukedom was merely a very belated recognition of his having borne the Sword at the Coronation of Charles II at Scone (the last Scottish Coronation) and having fought for him at Worcester.

It was in 1667 that Bruce, still not a Baronet of Nova Scotia, received his appointment as King's Surveyor in Scotland, and not until 1671 that he was officially entrusted with the task of rebuilding the Palace of Holyroodhouse, the actual contractual document, signed by Sir William Bruce of Balcaskie (Surveyor General of the King's Works), Sir William Sharpe of Stainiehill (King's Cash Keeper), and Robert Mylne (King's Master Mason), is dated 11th, and 12th, of March, 1672. The amount to be spent was £57,000 Scots, with Bruce's salary fixed at £3600 Scots, per annum (approximately £5000 and £300, in English money, respectively). Many amendments and additions followed, but this document firmly dates the present palace. It would appear, therefore, that while Bruce's contract for the work at Holyroodhouse may have been directly obtained through the influence of Lauderdale (who signed the termination document before work had completely ceased, and gave the Surveyorship to his brother, Lord Hatton, in 1679), neither he nor the Countess of Dysart seem to have had any particular hand in Bruce's being appointed King's Surveyor. This probably came quite naturally after his other appointments, and obviously resulted from his considerable reputation as the principlal architect in the Kingdom.

Nonetheless, having once got Bruce engaged by Royal Command on the rebuilding of Holyroodhouse the Lauderdales kept him busy throughout the 'seventies' of the seventeenth century on their own account, diverting men and materials to Thirlestane Castle, and Brunstane House, near Edinburgh, and to a minor extent Leithington; though John Maitland began to lose his resolve after his marriage to Eliza Murray (she was 'the boss' and he more the means whereby the King's ear, and approbation, could be obtained for personal plans). His own affairs, his Scottish houses, tended to fall into the background, and in any case there was Ham to rebuild and turn into the finest mansion of its kind and period in England (Evelyn rated it as fine as anything in Italy). Money poured out onto this, leaving in the end little for Scottish schemes, so that the Duke of Lauderdale was practically forced to 'borrow' Treasury funds to help pay for the enlargement and improvement of Brunstane, his Edinburgh home, and Thirlestane, his border seat, both of which Bruce undertook for him between 1672 and 1673; when work had already commenced at Holyrood. As a matter of fact even the Royal Secretary of State himself had his qualms on the subject of these diversions, for in his early correspondence with Bruce he enjoins secrecy over building plans, saying he will explain later.

In October 1672, in a letter written from Ham, the Duke of Lauderdale does explain;

> Now the reason why I recommended secrecy to you when I first called for the draught (Jan. 1671), was because I stood in awe of Sir William Sharpe, and was unwilling to give him an alarme before I had taken my resolutions; but now there is no remedy. I am resolved to build this summer, and therefore

you must adventure to tell him the whole matter. I hope he will not beat you, the worst is but a chiding and clawing of his lugg divers times, and calling where is the . . . cash, to which you shall answer him in my name, as Diego did in the play called the *Spanish Curate*, 'Even where you please, you are wise and know better where to get the money than I do.' This was Diego's answer when they asked him where the money was towards all the great legacies he had made, and this is my answer to Sir Wm. Sharpe as to the building of Brunstein, which I doubt must be built, and even this year too. But for his comfort the great building of Leidington shall stand untill first Thirlstein Castle, and secondly Brunstein be finished . . .

In the event the 'great building at Leidington,' was never done, and not surprisingly in view of how much was spent on the two previous ploys at Brunstane and Thirlestane. Indeed the heading to a letter sent in May 1671 by Lauderdale to his factor at Thirlestane: 'A new whimsey for enflaming the reckoning at Thirlestane Castle,' speaks volumes for his building mania, and his apprehension regarding its effect on others, 'being knockle deep in mortar I fear I shall be up to the elbows (if I live), before I have done with it,' he says, and ends, 'I send you this as ane entertainment for halfe a duson more pipes of tobacco.' The letter contains, incidentally, a tribute to Bruce's genius for solving awkward problems, for Lauderdale declares he is not troubled by 'the difficulties I object (because I know Sir Wm. Bruce has ane excellent faculty at all that).'

The correspondence switches at random from discussion on what concerned work done at Holyrood to that at Lauderdale's properties. A note of January 3rd, 1671 from Sir William Bruce, 'To the Earl of Lauderdaill at Whitehall, concerning the works at the Abbey and Thirlestane Castel,' is typical. It mentions how, 'Mr. Mylne (King's Mason), has promised nixt week to com hither and go with me to Thirlston Castle; he says the work advances well, and that he will do his pairt against the time condishended on. I am going about his Majesties work at Holyrudhous, and in a fue days I shall give your Lordship notice, if it will hold the draght and designe towards the east was spok of to his Majestie.' The language, grammar and spelling are not only odd but inconsistent. No 'norm' seems to have pertained at the time, each person, apparently, following their own particular inclinations. The work at Holyrood at this stage hardly amounted to much more than doing the necessary repairs and taking down temporary structural supports consequent upon the fire and other damage caused during the Cromwellian regime, plus the assembling of materials in preparation for the rebuilding which had yet to take place. The Lords Commissioners of the Treasury declared, in

February 1671, that; 'haveing spoak with Sir William Bruce there-anut (on the reparation of Holyroodhouse), wee find a necessitie for the present advance of one thousand punds sterling,' (£12,000 Scots). Quite a large sum considering.

Bruce's note of January 3rd 1671 is actually the very first document in which the question of restoring or rebuilding Holyroodhouse is specifically mentioned; and a full twelve months was to elapse before the final contract was signed. Robert Mylne, the mason with whom Sir William Bruce was to be associated on this and other jobs, was officially appointed King's Mason in succession to his uncle John in 1668, the same year in which Bruce himself was made a Baronet of Nova Scotia. John Mylne, 'Sixth Master Mason to a Royal Race of Seven successive Kings,' died in 1667 and lies buried in Greyfriars' Kirkyard, Edinburgh, below a handsome classical monument designed and erected by his nephew. Robert Mylne was practically the last of the line and the last of the true Royal Masons. The post lapsed with the advent of the Hanoverian dynasty and was only revived, in the case of Robert Reid (architect of St. George's Church, Charlotte Square, Edinburgh) in a purely honorary form by George IV. Robert Mylne's descendants were still trying to get payment for past arrears in the reign of the first George. Like Sir William Bruce he had been a servant of the native Royal House and had to suffer the consequences of its fall. He was Master Mason to Charles II, James VII and II, 'Williamanmary' (who neither dismissed him nor paid him) and Queen Anne. He died in 1710, shortly after Sir William Bruce.

On March 16th 1671 the Earl of Lauderdale wrote to Sir William Bruce asking him to send up sketch plans for Holyroodhouse for the King to see. The letter is jaunty in tone, referring to Bruce in one line as 'min Heer,' thanking him for various commissions done in Holland and, 'I cannot forget youre franc . . . journey in the year 1663,' a clear reference to earlier missions in search of *articles de vertue* on the Continent which Bruce was known to have accomplished. The King's Secretary for Scotland seems genuinely to have been solicitous for His Majesty's Surveyor's health as well, which appears to have been not too good at the time, for Lauderdale writes; 'Above all I am concerned by your health, and therefor I conjure you send me from your physician and surgeon ane exact relation of the progres and condition of your distemper and the remedies which have been applyed to the end I may returne you the best advice from this.' Such consideration tends to belie Bishop Burnet's estimation of Lauderdale's character, whom he described as 'the coldest friend and the most violent enemy that ever was known;' but it is true that as Duke and husband of Eliza Murray he did lose much of his former rough and ready native sense, and got gradually more and more out of touch with his old acquaintances, becoming a tool of his egotistical wife and no longer the originator of policies or anything else. His letter to Bruce ends; 'If you love me hasten this to me, for none can be more concerned in your recovery than is — Sir, your most affectionat and faithfull friend and servant, LAUDERDAILL.'

Not I think the sentiments of the coldest friend that was ever known, though possibly of the changed man who, in 1679, dismissed Bruce summarily from his post at Holyrood and handed the perquisites over to his own brother. Thus Burnet's comment about a violent enemy may be justified, but only as it applies to the days of Lauderdale's decline, when he helped his Duchess to be 'Besse of the Church and Besse of State,' to 'usurp both sceptre and crown' and 'destroy with a flap or her gown.' In 1644 the same 'Besse' was described as 'a very good harmless vertuouse witty little babe,' but no doubt her encounter with Old Noll, and some of the other unpleasant facts of life, altered all that, and only the wit she displayed in 1644 seems to have survived these experiences. That she brought out the worst in the Duke of Lauderdale can scarcely be gainsaid, it might even be thought he brought out the worst in her! They were certainly a most dangerous and none too likeable couple, though united not so much in the bed as the head.

The Duke was a prolific letter writer and a bit of a fuss-pot, and besides his frequent consultation of Sir William Bruce he laid many of his plans bare to his brother Charles Maitland, Lord Hatton. Two letters of April 1671 to Hatton are of some interest here as they concern, in one case, the possibility of the King's delay in making up his mind about what to do at Holyrood, and Lauderdale's fear that 'he will choose expensively and exhaust all the money before anything can be spent elsewhere.' The other throws more light on my lord Secretary's predilections, relating as it does to a bargain he made in London over some marble chimney-pieces, 'three of them are finer than any I see in England, and I have great pennieworth, two I have payed for this day, much finer than my Lord Chancellor's, larger and cheaper, above a fourth of his. I lighted on them by chance in ane Italian merchant's hand, who let me have them as he payed for them in Italie.'

Still in the month of April, 1671, Sir William Bruce, who seems to have been more or less permanently lodged in Edinburgh in those days, for all his letters are headed from the capital, received a note from cousin Bessie at Ham. It concerned the gateposts he was designing for her; not a vast commission but interesting because it proves he was definitely employed there, and quite early on, for the work of thorough reconstruction which the Countess was to inaugurate after becoming Duchess of Lauderdale did not begin in earnest until 1673, and was not complete outside until 1676. Whether or not it is possible to assess the character of Eliza Murray from her letter to Bruce is a moot point; it does not appear as transparent as Lauderdale's in his personal letters. Perhaps this is not a personal letter though it is to a relative, and someone whom the writer knows well. To me it seems as cold as Burnet suggests Lauderdale was; but in any case it is extremely precise and shows that both Duke and Duchess were very clear about what they wanted not only when it came to politics and influence but in architecture and furnishing.

'Sir' it begins; 'I desired E. Lauderdaill to lett you know that I like your Peers for the gate which you designed for me, therefore I desire you to proceed with the worke according to that figure . . . I am now at Ham so have considered of your proposal of making the gate only 12 feet wide, the great walk is 18 feet, so yet by your advice : the gate ought to be 3 feet on each side of the walk.' Then after giving further details on sizes, Lady Dysart comes to the cost of the gate itself, and whether or not it should be made in England or Scotland. She undoubtedly respects her architect cousin's judgement and asks; 'what do you think of making in each leaf of the Irongate a little wicket for ordinary use?' Then, possibly with a woman's intuition and realising she may be keeping Bruce from something else, she adds, 'I know you are at this time sufficiently employed, so that it is not very necessary to put you in mind of what concerns your friends, which makes me seldom trouble you. I shall be glad to know how you do in your health when you write to me. I beseech you present my more humble service to your lady, — I am, most faithfully your affectionate cossen to your humble servants. E. DYSART.' Her spelling is better than either Lauderdale's or Bruce's. Possibly the fact that her father was a clergyman and had been the intimate of the most cultured and fastidious of princes, King Charles I, had something to do with that; and Lady Bruce is mentioned. We hear very little of her in these letters, while hers, all of a family nature, are more interesting later on, when she visited London for the Coronation of James VII and II and Mary of Modena, and sent back to Kinross an account of the firework display and other jollifications on that occasion.

The drawings of the proposed new Palace at Holyroodhouse, which Lauderdale asked for in his letter of March 16th 1671 evidently arrived soon afterwards, for on June 3rd of the same year, Charles II, who does not seem to have delayed as long in his decision as Lauderdale hinted he might, issued the necessary Royal Warrant for work to begin on the Palace and Chapel. The complete text appears in *The Master Masons to the Crown of Scotland*, by the late Rev.

9   Balcaskie. Northern facade showing duplication
of original tower, left and right, and new entrance
feature

10   Forecourt at Balcaskie, with new wing walls
and part side pavilion

11   Detail of wing wall at Balcaskie. The niches
formerly contained busts of Roman Emperors, now
on garden terrace buttresses

12   Bruce's 'Italian' terrace overlooking the
Firth of Forth

13 Ceiling in older part of Balcaskie, the so-called 'Globe Room' (1665–70)

14 Fretwork ceiling by George Dunsterfield in the Library (1674)

15 Southern front at Balcaskie showing early attempts at symmetry. First floor windows and balcony date from 18th and 19th centuries

16 Ham House, Richmond. Home of the Duke and
Duchess of Lauderdale. Note wing wall and niches
containing busts of Emperors and contemporary rulers

17 Brunstane House, the Lauderdale's villa near
Edinburgh. West front showing old house on left.
Connecting porch modern

Thirlestane Castle, Berwickshire as completed. Oriel windows and conical turrets 19th century

19 Detail entrance

Side view showing adaptation of curious old round towers and Border 'keep'

21 Detail of 'Germane' work in ante-room at
Thirlestane (1671–2)

22 Elaborate fretwork ceiling in the ballroom by
Halbert and Dunsterfield, 'gentlemen modellers'

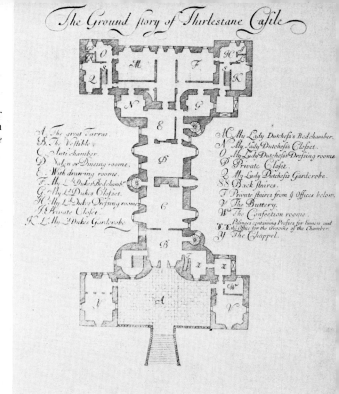

The Ground story of Thirlestane Castle

A. The great Tarras.
B. The Vestible.
C. Anti chamber.
D. Salon or Dineing roome.
E. With drawing roome.
F. My Ld Dukes Bedchambr.
G. My Ld Dukes Closet.
H. My Ld Dukes Dressing roome.
J. Private Closet.
K. My Ld Dukes Garderobe.

M. My Lady Dutchess's Bedchamber.
N. My Lady Dutchess's Closet.
O. My Lady Dutchess's Dressing roome.
P. Private Closet.
Q. My Lady Dutchess's Garderobe.
SS. Back stairs.
T. Private staires from ye Offices below.
V. The Buttery.
W. The Confection roome.
X. Passages containing Presses for linnen and the Office for the dressing of the Chamber.
Y. The Chappel.

23 Plan of Ground Floor
at Thirlestane Castle from
Theatrum Scotiae

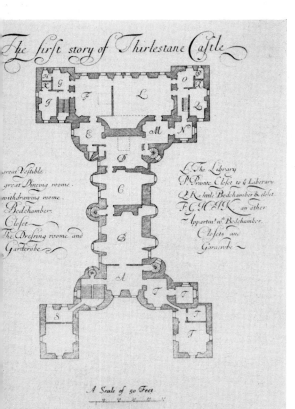

The first story of Thirlestane Castle

...great Vestible
...great Dineing roome.
...withdrawing roome.
...Bedchamber.
...Closet
...The Dressing roome and
...Garderobe

L. The Library
P. Private Closet to ye Library
Q. Related Bedchamber & closet
F.G.H.J.K. an other
Appartm'nt Bedchamber.
Closets and
Garderobe

A Scale of 50 Feet

24 Plan of First Story

25   Lauder Kirk, detail of
tower

26   The kirk in its setting.
      Compare Balleroy

Robert Scott Mylne, I will not repeat it all here but try and pick out the salient points. It is addressed principally to the 'Lords Commissioners of our Treasury in Scotland,' by 'Charles R.,' who, 'having seriously perused the plan of the ground together with the drawght of our intended Palace of Holyroodhouse, doe here inclosed send you our directions for purchasing adjacent grounds . . . as also such alterations as wee doe judge convenient; in pursueance of which wee doe by these presents authorise you to proceed in the purchase of the grounds and houses belonging to the Bishop and Dean of Edinburgh . . . and legally securing an equivalent yearly value to the Bishop and Dean and their successors in due forme of law; which when you have finished, wee will signe the securityes as you send them up, and take good care to have them ratified in the next Session of our Parliament.' This smacks of the true Charles who was determined 'not to be sent on his travels again.' Continuing, the King declares : 'As to the alterations wee propose in the outer fabrick and disposeing of the apartments, you shall returne to us your opinions after advice with Sr Wm. Bruce, whom wee have commissioned to be our Generall Surveyor of the whole works at the said Palace, and such other of our Castles and Palaces as wee shall give order to have repaired. And you shall make due payment of the salary which wee have granted him yeerly and termly until wee shall discharge the same, and that out of the moneys granted to us by the late Session of Parliament; for all which this shall be to yow a sufficient warrant; and soe wee bid yow heartily farewell. Given at our Court at Windesor Castle, the third day of June 1671 and our reigne the 23rd year. — By his Majesties Command. LAUDERDAILL.

Holyrood was a semi-religious foundation, hence the ecclesiastical connections remaining at the time of Charles II, handed down from the pre-Reformation Abbots to secular Commendators and finally to the Episcopal Bishop and Dean of Edinburgh. In fact, like so many ancient residences of the kind (one thinks particularly of Hampton Court and Windsor) which grew and were not planned, portions were rented or 'farmed out' to private persons many of whom were difficult to get rid of when the time came for the Crown to assert its overall ownership. One of the contemporary letters dealing with the rebuilding of Holyrood and other palaces and castles in Scotland refers to the King's desire to purchase the hereditary right of the Earl of Mar to be Keeper of the Castle at Stirling, H.M's principal fortalice in his northern Kingdom, the possible exclusion from which, by a subject, though theoretically possible would seem in practice ridiculous. Charles did not, incidentally, succeed in his desires, and not only Stirling but Falkland as well still have hereditary Keepers who could, if they so chose, lock themselves in until removed by force.

In the case of Holyrood, private property abounded within and without; there was still the House of the Commendator, built in the most awkward place imaginable, right in front of the West Door of the Abbey from which the original foundation derived. This domestic dwelling remained even after Bruce had finished rebuilding the palace alongside and restoring the Abbey behind and was only removed in the eighteenth century, when all possibility of a King ever coming to stay in the palace seemed over. Indeed the place was left more or less to the Dukes of Hamilton, Hereditary Keepers of Holyroodhouse and the providers, believe it or not, of much of the existing furniture in the old historic quarters nowadays shown to visitors. The State Apartments, however, were furnished largely by the late Queen Mary, the first member of the present Royal House to take the slightest interest in their principal Scottish Residence since the departure of James, Duke of York in 1683. Prince Charles held his famed ball in the Long Gallery there in 1745, and a year later 'Butcher Cumberland' slept in Queen Mary's bed, not Mary, Queen of Scots, as the guides tell you, but Mary of Modena, Queen of James VII and II, when Duchess of York; but neither of these visitations were more than fleeting, as was the imitatory descent upon the poor old house by 'Prinney' and his friends in 1822. Some of the ladies then presented to 'Highland Geordie' could remember as girls curtseying to his distant cousin, the *de jure* King Charles III, in the same setting. One wonders what their thoughts were, and what unflattering comparisons were made. Charles X of France stayed at Holyrood on and off after the Revolution of 1789, and again following his own abdication in 1830. Queen Victoria did not normally stay there, nor Edward VII, both were the guests of the Duke of Buccleuch (the direct descendant of Charles II and Lucy Walters) at Dalkeith Palace. Charles II never visited Holyrood, he probably never intended to, and the work carried out after the Restoration was really part of accepted Restoration policy, that is, to fulfil so far as possible Charles I's will, to restore what had been destroyed or removed during the civil war and complete that which had already been begun beforehand. A note pinned to the copy of John Mylne's plans of Holyrood (made for Charles I when Mylne was that discerning monarch's Master Mason), states; 'This was His Majesties blessed fatheres intentione in anno 1633.'

The old Abbey was founded by David I of Scots, a son of Queen Margaret, and usually referred to in history books as, 'that sair sanct for the croun', on account of his inordinate piety and pre-occupation with the founding of abbeys and monasteries. The legend of the Holy Rood is virtually the same as that of St. Eustace, who went hunting on a Sunday only to be met in the woods by a strange stag, white and with a rood, or crucifix between its antlers, which brought on a fit of remorse. Substitute King David of Scots for St. Eustace and you have in essence the story concocted by the monks of Holyrood in the mid-fourteenth century to save the face of David II, son of Robert the Bruce, who lost the real Holy Rood (Queen Margaret's ebony and ivory crucifix which had been Scotland's talisman since the eleventh century) at the Battle of Neville's Cross in 1346. From the twelfth to the fifteenth centuries the Abbey of the Holy Rood existed as a purely ecclesiastical entity. The Scottish Kings, and especially the Stewarts, were all rather pious, some would say almost super-stitious; they did not build for themselves royal residences as such until the sixteenth century, preferring to reside in or near some abbey or monastery. Scone was one, Stirling another (with the Abbey of Cambuskenneth clearly visible in the plain below the castle); and so, in the end, was Holyroodhouse, which actually grew as an extension to the existing monastic buildings, inheriting in the process the name and story associated with the religious foundation.

I mentioned the Abbey of Cambuskenneth just now, and it is significant for two reasons; it was largely built by Alexander Mylne, its mason-Abbot in the fifteenth century, and it was the burial place of James III, who initiated the royal connection with Holyrood Abbey. Perhaps the most obviously pious and artistic of the earlier Stewarts James was the first Scottish king to make Edinburgh his main residence, and because he did not like living in the castle spent much of his time at the Abbey, in the hospice for visitors, which became, through this royal association, the nucleus of what his son, James IV, turned into a secular Royal Palace. In fact, the fourth James planned the facade more or less on similar lines to those adopted by Bruce in 1672, though he only completed one of the characteristic Renais-sance towers (to the north) Bruce being responsible for the other.

James IV engaged Walter Merlioun, a Frenchman, as his Supervisor-Mason at Holyrood, but a member of the Mylne family was also on the job. In fact the palace had a Mylne working on it at every stage till the last, when Robert Mylne finished it for Charles II. James V undertook many improvements, mostly inside, as he was anxious to please his two French Queens, Madeleine of France (daughter of François Premier), who died shortly after her arrival in Scotland, and Mary of Guise, sister of the Duke of Lorraine and Cardinal de Guise one of the highest born and most influential princesses of her day. The interior of the northern tower, which outside already resembled part of a Chateau by the Loire, was decorated in the current French taste of blue and gold. Some of this remains, plus the mono-grams and ensignia of James V and Mary of Guise, and of their daughter, Mary, Queen of Scots and her husband, the Dauphin

François. The floor levels in this older part of Holyrood, however, were altered by Bruce and apart from the splendid ceiling with its Franco-Scottish armorial devices very little of the pre-Union Palace of the old Stewart Kings has survived. The Abbey was what they call 'disaffected' in 1560, the choir was allowed to fall down and only the nave was still used, as a parish church.

James IV's original plan never fully materialised, even in the century after his death. James VI had a scheme for getting things moving again, but when he became first King of Great Britain, Scotland and what happened there, lost importance. Thus it was left to Charles I to resurrect the idea of making Holyrood a worthy place as a Royal Residence. John Mylne, his Master Mason, was charged with revising the plans and making new drawings, and building new facades in which the Whitehall - Inigo Jones style predominated. A proportion of this work was actually begun before the Civil War broke out, when it had to be abandoned; and a fire during the Cromwellian occupation put paid to it altogether. At least the restored Abbey was spared; in it King Charles had been crowned, and Jones himself is said to have been responsible for the early-Gothic-revival West front with its somewhat over confident inscription:

HE SHALL BUILD ANE HOUSE
FOR MY NAME, AND I WILL
STABLISH THE THRONE
OF HIS KINGDOM
FOR EVER

The most interesting part of King Charles's revision of his great-grandfather's plan was the extension of the main frontage by a third bay, beginning with the existing ancient tower, making a linking gallery, then another similar tower, a further gallery and then a third tower. This of course showed the Martyr King's appreciation of good proportion, for it was he who suggested the extension, which, had it been done, would have rendered Holyroodhouse superior to all other palaces and residences in the United Kingdom in grace and classical perfection. Charles I's scheme was perhaps too ambitious, more on the scale of his proposals for Whitehall, on which Inigo Jones spent so much time on. It would have provided, amongst other things, for a double courtyard, where Bruce only provided one, and many more outbuildings and embellishments in the garden and immediate surroundings; but Charles I himself levied, and collected the taxes in the realm, and if he could not always really afford many of his cultural schemes it was rarely that they suffered. More usually it was something like the army that had to go short. Charles II did not recover his father's freedom in this respect, at least not until he made himself a pensioner on Louis XIV and was able to ignore a stingy parliament; by which time the restoration of palaces only mattered if they immediately affected his own personal comfort, and Holyrood never came into that category.

Still, at the Restoration it was fully intended that the plans drawn up by John Mylne for King Charles I would be carried out, and it is possible that had Mylne survived a little longer, or a firm decision been taken regarding the implementation of the pre-Restoration design before he died in 1667, we should have seen a more marvellous Holyrood than even Bruce produced. Mylne himself was no amateur either, he it was who restored the Abbey for the King of blessed memory, and he it was who, after being sent by the King to study the crown steeple at Newcastle (the only Medieval one left intact, and whose construction, therefore, could be with safety, copied), rebuilt the original crown steeple of St. Giles. It was John Mylne who designed and built the Tron Kirk, near St. Giles, an unique northern essay based on St. Eustache in Paris;[1] and again, was responsible for completing Parliament Hall, with its wonderful pendant-key roof, in time for Charles I to open the Estates in person on his Coronation visit of 1633. No wonder his grave stone in Greyfriars is so fulsome;

MAJESTIC MAN FOR PERSON, WIT, AND GRACE
THIS GENERATION CANNOT FILL HIS PLACE.
It is possibly also worth recalling that Robert Mylne, who did build Holyrood (according to Sir William Bruce's drawings), and who designed his uncle's tombstone, had this epitaph set up;
HERE LYES THE FAMOUS ROBERT MILNE
LAIRD OF BALFARGIE, WHO HAD MORE SKILL
IN MASON CRAFT HIMSELF ALONE
THAN MOST HIS BRETHREN JOINED IN ONE.

The Mylne papers mention the existence in the Bodleian Library in Oxford of a copy, dated 1663, of he original scheme for Holyrood. It is this copy which bears the reference to Charles I's intentions, sealed in wax to the drawings. These plans are stated to have been surveyed by 'John Mylne, his Majestie's Mr. Messone.' The next set of drawings are those referred to in Lauderdale's letter to Sir William Bruce of March 16th 1671, which formed the basis of the contract drawn up between Bruce, Sharp and Robert Mylne at that time. They include a sketch of the Palace as it had come down from posterity, unfinished and only partially habitable, consisting of the Abbey Church and adjacent Palace of James IV and James V. That is, one northern tower and half the gallery stretching towards an unbuilt southern replica. Bruce continued this elevation much as it was, added the balancing southernmost tower, and planted his entirely new Palladian edifice on behind.

This was the general revised layout which the King approved on the 'third day of June 1671,' and confirmed by Royal Warrant. The plans were later modified in some particulars, I will deal with these in my next chapter, suffice to say here that the Chapel which Bruce showed as being in his replica tower (to the south), was discarded, and Charles decided he would instead use the Abbey Kirk, to which a loft or gallery would open from the house; 'His Majestie will have noe Chapell in this new house, but ane entrie from the Guarde Chamber on the Royall Apartment towards the East into the Church, and his private family prayers in or near the Presence as in Whitehall.' There were other royal criticisms of Bruce's plan, in fact, item 7 of H.M's directions begins: 'His Majestie does noe way approve of three Royal Appartments, they being absolutely unnecessary;' and further on, 'His Majestie does alsoe much dislike his Privy Gallery . . . he likes not the covering of all that betwixt the two Great toures with platform at the second Storie, but would have it heightended to a third Storie' (this was not done, the centre gallery between the two towers was pulled down and rebuilt in the Doric Order, with cupola and Imperial Crown above, as seen today).

The King did like the general layout, however, and added an interesting memo about chimneys. 'His Majestie likes very well to have chimneys in the corners of roomes where it is not soe convenient to sett them in any of the sides and hath made his new House at New Markett with all the chimneys in the corners.' John Evelyn notes Charles II's fondness for corner chimneys in an entry in his *Diary* relating to a visit he made to Newmarket in 1670. 'Many of the rooms had chimneys in the angles and corners, a mode now introduced by his Majesty, which I do at no hand approve of.' Evelyn did not approve of a lot of things, and it was not, I suppose, a good idea to put corner chimneys in every room, including large ones, as apparently Charles did, it spoilt the proportion; but the information that the 'Merry Monarch' himself introduced this particular fashion is significant, as it not only disproves theories that Wren brought corner chimneys into the country at the behest of Queen Mary, consort of William of Orange, so that she could display her blue-and-white china better (a visit to Hampton Court would reveal what is meant), but it helps to explain Bruce's early use of the mode. There are corner chimneys at both Kinross and at Hopetoun.

William Adam, who is generally assumed to have been apprenticed to Sir William Bruce at some stage in his very early career, made a set of drawings of Holyroodhouse as designed and built under the supervision of the King's Architect and Surveyor. They appear in his *Vitruvius Scoticus*, at the beginning, and make an authentic record of what was eventually done. The first drawings, upon which Charles commented so freely and which are reproduced in *The King's Master Masons*, were made by Robert Mylne himself, for the King, and have been preserved for posterity by the Master Mason's descendants. That Charles II, normally thought of as lazy and indulgent, spent a considerable time digesting the content of these plans is obvious, and that his critical eye was both well trained and reliable cannot be denied when one reads through what he had to say. Furthermore, having had his say, he leaves room neither for delay nor misunderstanding; 'It is his Majesties pleasure that the Lords Commissioners of his Treasury consider these alterations and directions with the advice of Sir William Bruce and returne ane answer accordingly, yet that preparations be made, and the work goe on with all speedy dispatche possible; And that a full Drawght of the whole Designe be sent to the King soe soone as it can conveniently be made ready.

These orders were read againe to his Majestie and approved.' The signature is Lauderdale's; but there can be no doubt of the King's frequent and knowledgeable amendment of the text as submitted by His Secretary for Scotland.

[1] The link between the Legend of St. Eustace and that of Edinburgh's Holyrood would seem here to be further confirmed.

Orleans wing; Chateau de Blois

CHAPTER FOUR

Brunstane, Thirlestane and the completion of Holyroodhouse

WORK ACTUALLY BEGAN on the rebuilding of Holyrood in July 1671, when Sir William Bruce was ordered to take down the iron grilles which must have been over the windows since late medieval times, 'and with all possible diligence he make effectual and speedy provision of stone lime timber Iron, glasse, and all other necessaries for that work in the most frugall way and to the best advantage he can. He observing in all his Majesties directions and orders of which just doubles are herewith delivered to him.' With the same command Bruce was instructed to repair 'his Majesties Castle of Sterling,' including the roof, wright work and glass work, this to be finished by the first of November of the same year. The King's Architect was also to 'take care to provide all necessaries for making up Ship carriages for the Canon in the said Castle, the provision and Workmanship being left to his care as above.' The stone dyke at Stirling was to be effectively repaired, 'and for the speedy perfecting of it he shall make the best bargain he can.'

What a busy man Bruce must have been, and what an immense amount of reliance was put on his skill and judgement by his royal and noble superiors! It must have been bad enough the King wanting so many things changed, and the Lords of the Treasury being so pernickety about money and small details, but worse than this surely was Lauderdale's constant mention of his own private ploys. Even the letter saying he is about to dispatch the King's formal orders for the rebuilding of Holyrood contains more comment about Thirlestane than the proposed new palace; and the haste to repair Stirling may in part be traced to Lauderdale's wish that too much is not spent on it, and to his desire to get it ready before attempting the rather tricky task of ousting the Earl of Mar from his post as hereditary keeper. Writing to Lord Hatton from Ham, two days after sending another letter about the work at Holyrood and his design for 'the great roome at Thirlestane Castle,' the King's Scottish Secretary refers to his

The West Front of the Royal Palace of Holy-rood House tons

Duke of Corn

Sr Wm Bruce Arch!
...Adam delin.

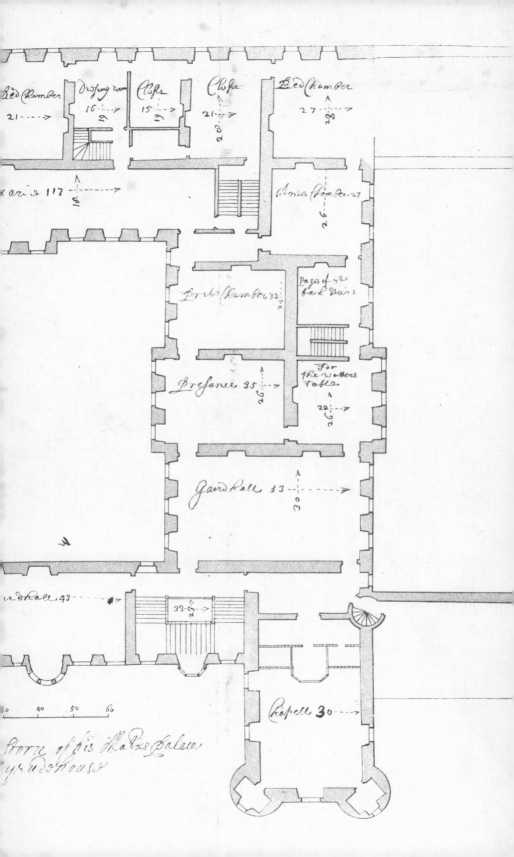

Bed Chamber 21 --->

Drssing room 16 ---> 19

Clofs 15 ---> 19

Clofer 21 --> 20

Bed Chamber 27 ---> 28

arie 117 ---> 10

Anie Chamber 27 9

Drub Chamber 32 27

Page of 42 back staire

Prefonce 35 ---> 26

For the waiters table 22 ---> 26

Gaurd Ralle 53 ---> 30

ard Ralle 43 ----->

33 27 --->

Chapell 30 --->

30 40 50 60

floore of his Matie Palace
yr udohouse

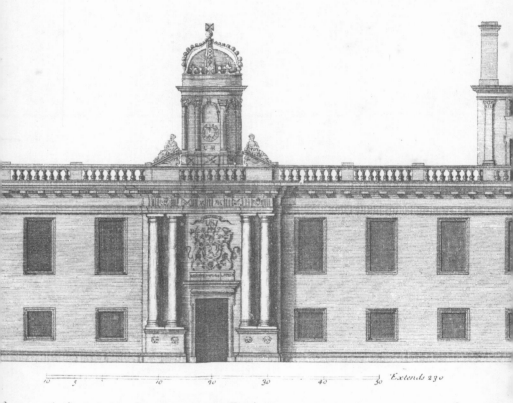

10 5   10   20   30   40   50 Extends 230

~~urt with the Plans and other Fronts of this Royal Palace. Is most humbly Inscrib'd~~
~~hefter. High Steward of Scotland, Duke of Edinburgh & Knight of the most Noble Order of~~

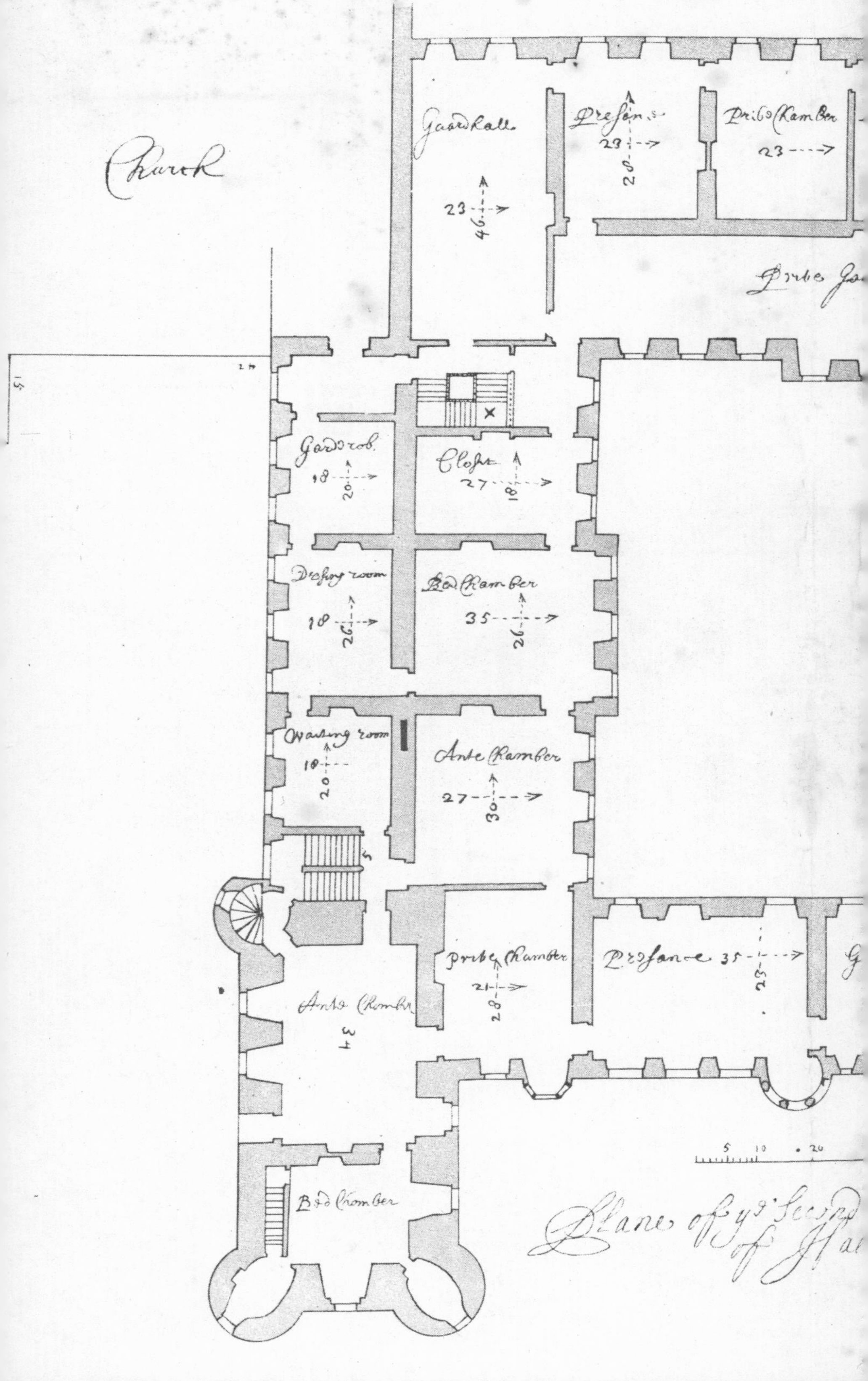

Church

GuardHall

Presen.
23
20

Priu Chamber
23

23
64

Priue Ga

Gardrob.
18
20

Cloßt
27
81

X

Dreßing room
18
22

Bed Chamber
35
26

Waiting room
18
20

Ante Chamber
27
30

Ante Chamber
34

Priue Chamber
21
28

Preßance
35
35

G

Bed Chamber

5 10   20

Plane of ye Second
of Hall

To His Royal Highness FREDERICK Prince of Wales,

he Garter &c.

R. Cooper sculp.

Majesties command 'to endeavour to buy from the Earl of Mar his heritable right of keeping the Castle of Sterling.' Charles thought it quite unreasonable that the place should be in the hands of any subject by inheritance. 'I told his Majestie,' goes on Lauderdale, 'It would be very deare if he offered to buy it, the grandfather of the Earle got two thousand pounds for the heritable right of keeping the Castle of Edinburgh . . . and this, if well guided oght to be much cheaper, for this Earle Marr is low and wants money and hath no child.' The King apparently approved of the idea of putting the matter in the hands of Lord Hatton, who is beseeched to do the best he can to persuade the Earl 'to offer to sell, even to the King.'

As if this was not enough to be going on with, Lauderdale now announced he was to be made Governor of the Bass Rock, which, in September 1671, Sir William Bruce would be asked to survey and repair (it had a fort and prison built on it) 'before next winter.'[1] Ham too features in the same month's correspondence. Evidently Lauderdale was beginning to get into a tizzy about his dear Bessie's gates, for he entreats his brother to 'tell Sir Wm. Bruce from me that I much desire the hastening of C. Dysart's gate. The King and Queen will be hear this summer (the letter is dated June 1671). It will be a shame not to have the gate up, and hasten notice whether the Iron gates for it can be made in Scotland or not.' Finally, on July 27th, Lord Kincardine, one of the Lords Commissioners for Scotland, a cousin of Sir William Bruce and grandson of Sir George Bruce of Culross, wrote to Lauderdale to confirm that Robert Mylne has been alerted to begin the mason work at Holyrood after completing a few running repairs and assembling the requisite amount of scaffolding. 'He is to have 2000 deals and 500 trees to the bargaine . . . L. H. (Lord Hatton), Will Bruce and I thinke of going Saturday to see Thirlston Castle.'

The legal document, or Contract, for the rebuilding of Holyrood, was, as already mentioned, drawn up and signed in Edinburgh in favour of Sir William Bruce (Architect) Sir William Sharpe (Cash Keeper) and Robert Mylne (Mason) on the 11th and 12th of March 1672;the total expenditure to be £57,000 (Scots), or about £5000 (Sterling). One of the witnesses, it may be of interest, was Sir Thomas Moncreiffe of 'yt ilke,' who signed for Robert Mylne at the Canongate on March 12th. Bruce signed on the previous day, and was witnessed by a Writer to the Signet and his clerk. Between March and October there is no further correspondence, so one must assume that Lauderdale was too busy settling in as second husband of 'C. Dysart' at Ham and enjoying his new Dukedom. His first wife, Anne Home, daughter and co-heir of the first Earl of Home, died in January, and he was wed to Lady Dysart six weeks later, in

February. Sir George Mackenzie,[2] 'Bluidy Mackenzie' as he was called by the Covenanters on account of his strict interpretation of the law against treason and violence, records that Lauderdale 'really yielded to his gratitude, she having formerly saved his life by her mediation with the Usurper (Oliver Cromwell). There was indeed a fairly general belief among her contemporaries that she had been Cromwell's mistress.' The Duke, as he now became, 'had acted with much steadiness and uniformity before,' declared Bishop Burnet, 'but at this time there happened a great alteration in his temper, occasioned by the humours of a profuse, imperious woman . . . '

Certainly the letters to Bruce, Hatton and the rest temporarily dried up and did not commence again in anything like their former profusion until the end of October, when the question of Thirlestane and enlarging Brunstane (former home of his first wife) cropped up in a letter to the King's Architect and Surveyor. 'I mean to finish Brunstein first of all, after Thirlestane Castle, and let Lethington stand a blow till the park dyke be finished and all the copses planted . . . Doe you therefore haste to me the draught of Brunstein Offices and all, with all speed you can, to the end I may send you my positive resolution this winter, for I mean to build these next summer, and none shall know till I send you my positive orders. Finish on any terms your bargane for the bridge there, also the Avenue planted, and hasten to me the draught of Brunstein. Adieu.'

Poor Bruce! I wonder how much of Dame Mary he saw in those days, how often and for how long he was able to stay at Balcaskie, enjoy the company of his son and daughter, John and Anne, or visit neighbours, let alone examine work going on in Perthshire and elsewhere north of the Forth? I imagine most of the time he stayed in Edinburgh, at his 'ludgings' in the High Street, along with other notabilities. The 'Royal Mile' was then still the hub of Scottish society, all living on the 'common stair,' from those who governed the country to potters, fishwives and merchants. With Holyrood on his plate, however, as well as many smaller jobs in the country, it must have been quite a business fulfilling the demands of his patrons at Ham. Thirlestane alone was a major work, and now at Brunstane there was to be created a 'handsome villa' and park for his lordship. The house is little known and stands in the midst of an odd stretch of 'green belt' half way between Edinburgh and Musselburgh, behind the houses so to speak, and virtually encircled by an assortment of coal bings, electric pylons and similar excretia of the industrial age. On the other hand it is so interesting a design and has survived so well that I am surprised more notice has not been taken of it and some scheme of careful restoration not undertaken. It obviously delighted Lauderdale for his acknowledgment of the receipt of Bruce's drawings in the Autumn of 1671 is unequivocal on the subject; 'I was very well pleased with your draught of Brunstein.'

Brunstane comes in much the same category as Balcaskie, and to a lesser extent Holyroodhouse itself, in that it was a reconstruction and extension of an existing older building, the required symmetry and proportion being provided by the same simple espedient Bruce had employed at his own house in Fife by repeating part of the original structure a short distance away and joining the two up by a linking entrance wing. The first Brunstane seems to have been, again like Balcaskie, an 'L' shaped Laird's tower, probably built about the middle of the sixteenth century. In it the Maitlands had dwelt when they wished to be nearer Edinburgh than either Leithington or Thirlestane, and the date over the door, together with the quartered arms of Lauderdale and Home, is 1639. Bruce made the house a double 'L' instead of a single one, and drove an arched pend through to the garden, so that circulation must have been entirely on the first floor, where the finest rooms were. Some still are, including the Duke of Lauderdale's former library, with its daring bridge and steps leading out of a French window down to the garden below. The avenue mentioned in the Duke's letter can just be made out by the present straggle of a few mangy looking trees. It ran directly from the squared forecourt towards the west, crossing a bridge, (now referred to as being of Roman origin) which Bruce built for his client in 1672/3. The vista here takes in Arthur's seat, below which Holyrood stands, while in the opposite direction it looks over the Firth of Forth to the hills of Fife. The whole effect must have been particularly agreeable before the estate was enclosed by factories and railways and inter-war housing.

Lord Milton, a nephew of Alexander Fletcher of Saltoun (the Scottish patriot and opponent of the Union of Parliaments in 1707) rented Brunstane in the eighteenth century and it was he who had the elaborate baroque plasterwork done over chimneypieces and elsewhere. This was the work of itinerant *stuccatore*, possibly the same ones who were engaged by William Adam at 'The Drum,' Gilmerton, a mile or two to the south, and at Newhailes, which is the adjoining estate to Brunstane. 'The Drum,' though a Stewart mansion as to foundation, is largely William Adam as seen today, and was built by this famous pupil of Bruce after an architectural tour conducted by Sir John Clerk of Penicuik, for whom Adam had worked as mason. It is a much smaller building and less demonstrative outside than most of William Adam's, but inside the hall and dining room are a riot of curves and trophies, 'umbrella stands' of swords and spears, freizes of fruit and vegetables, the bills for which are extant. The same Italians who decorated 'The Drum,' (they were probably

Italians, not Dutchmen as Sacheverell Sitwell, in his *British Architects and Craftsmen*, and John Fleming, in *Scottish Country Houses Open to the Public*, aver),[3] went on to embellish neighbouring Newhailes, the home of the erudite and able Scottish Judge, Lord Hailes.

From Newhailes it is but a short walk over the fields to Brunstane where, in Bruce's splendid octagonal room, the *stuccatore* set up the Fletcher of Saltoun Achievement in plaster amidst the usual assortment of arms, martial equipment and vegetation, and this remains *in situ*. The octagonal room itself is one of Bruce's masterpieces, possibly inspired by something seen abroad, but predating similar work at Ham. Its chaste and beautiful panelling is serenely Palladian showing only the barest suggestion of baroque in the lugged corners of the door architraves, and sizeable rounded mouldings of the chimneypiece; while the 'chassie,' or sash windows are probably the very first ever hung in Scotland. They may have been the work of joiners sent up from Ham and described variously as Dutch or 'Germane' by Lauderdale, but more likely Dutch in view of the great taste and precision shown, for sash windows were a Dutch speciality, not a German one, indeed, apart from Britain and the Netherlands, they are now nowhere else seen in any great number except in Portugal and Turkey. The Turkish connotation is purely fortuitous and has nothing to do with the present context, the Portugese connection may be more important since the Queen, Catherine of Braganza, came from Portugal, and a certain amount of baroque furniture and 'exotica' followed in her train (there was a 'Portugall' bed at Ham, for instance); and of course the use of tropical woods and other materials from Brazil and India which resulted from this marriage must have played a part in enriching Restoration taste.

The Royal Commission on Ancient Monuments speaks very highly of this octagonal room at Brunstane, going so far as to suggest that the 'chassie' windows there are literally the same as they were when put in for the Duke of Lauderdale by Bruce in 1673. A close examination will show this to be not literally the case, but near enough, the characteristically heavy moulded astragals are in evidence throughout and in one window the original seventeenth century glass has survived unrepaired! Over the doors in the corners are painted panels, the work, very likely, of Netherlandish artists sent north from Ham, where they painted similar scenic panels, only these at Brunstane are said to represent Scottish scenes. It is not easy to be sure of this, because they are so dark. A judicious cleaning might help to clear up the point. Unless they were painted after 1675, however, which is unlikely, they could not have been done by either Dirck van den Bergen (a pupil of one of the Van de Veldes who painted nineteen inset panels at Ham), or Abraham Jansz Begeyn, both of whom arrived in Britain after that date. This means that the Brunstane panels were probably painted by a predecessor, no doubt one of the anonymous Continental artists mentioned in the guide book to Ham who specialised in pastoral landscapes, seascapes, plants and animals, 'early in the seventies.' The fashion for this kind of work lasted quite a long time, at any rate in Scotland. There are some good examples at Caroline Park (circa 1696), not I think, a Bruce design but built and finished by craftsmen trained by him at Holyrood, and at Auchendinny (1703–07), which is the last built of the authenticated Bruce houses still standing more or less as he designed it.

In view of the completeness of Brunstane and its novelty for its time (its comforts were the very latest and installed before the more renowned ones at Ham), I think it worth quoting extensively from the correspondence about it between Lauderdale and Sir William Bruce, for it was upon Brunstane that both Bruce and his employer lavished a great deal of attention and care, discussing and deliberating over every small detail in a quite extraordinary way. Had the furnishings of the house remained intact as the house itself has, and as they have done at Ham (where the inventory of 1679 lists three quarters of the present contents of that unique Restoration residence), Brunstane would probably be the most interesting seventeenth century house in Scotland. Melville, in Fife, the possible creation of James Smith, working under the influence of Bruce, used to be complete down to its famous State bed, until everything was sold, the bed going to the Victoria and Albert Museum, the rest, who knows where? Now Scotland can no longer boast a true counterpart to Ham, at least not in respect of furnishings or furniture, though the garden at Kinross survives.

A week after the Duke of Lauderdale had asked to see Sir William Bruce's 'draught of Brunstein Offices' in October 1672, another letter followed explaining precisely what he, the Duke, intended to do. On plans previously prepared by Bruce, Lauderdale made alterations, explaining that he could not have done so earlier 'until first I knew my mind about it, nor had I even time to consider it thoroughly, until after the Earl of Kincardine and my brother were gone' (this is the same letter in which the reasons for secrecy over the first drawing came out, and Lauderdale says he stands in awe of Sir Wm. Sharpe). 'Then I came hither (Ham), and drew this draught which I here send you to be considered, together with your own original draft, of all which I have kept copies so that we may convers upon the alterations without sending drafts any more. Now I will answer your letter and then give you the reasons of my alterations. In the first place, I do not intend a house of much receite, and, therefore, though I like the seat very well . . . I will by no means build a fine house there. I mean, God-willing, to pursue the design of the gardens , . . and that same designe for the house which you and I first agreed upon.' Here follow a number of details which are almost impossible of comprehension without the plans referred to, the main point concerning the Duke's great Chamber, which Bruce turned to the west, and which didn't please Lauderdale because the windows would face onto the court and not have a decent view : 'therefore I am resolved to turn the great Chamber to the east side, where I shall have fair lights looking upon the sea and upon Fife.' He did not like the dining room either, which he says 'is miserably little . . . and so I should be forced to eate constantly in the second story, which would keep it always nasty.' A refinement rather unexpected in so coarse a man, at such a barbarous period and in so supposedly backward a land. Foreign travel seems to have softened not only Bruce's corners but Lauderdale's as well!

The pend leading right under the house from the court to the garden, which prevented proper circulation on the ground floor and later caused Lord Milton to build a linking corridor in front and block up the old passageway, was Lauderdale's own idea; 'I shall gain my beloved little low gallery,' he writes, 'which, though you despise because of the lownes and the narrowness, yet I shall like well as a good passage to the garden, where I will have a billiard-board and other conveniences.' Further details are followed by, 'And now let me describe to you this draught which I send you . . . A) is my little gallery, B) an anti-room to the parlour, D) my low parlour, C) my tobacco-room, E) the great stairs (there are none today, only two turnpikes, which makes one wonder if the big ones were ever built), 'F) a dining-room for my steward and waiters, I) a buttery, K) for keeping candlesticks, brooms etc. As to the kitchen-court, a room for the meanest servants to eate in.' A list of rooms on the second floor includes the great Chamber and various bedrooms, one of which is to be enlarged by making a corner chinmey. A year later Brunstane has not been built, and new correspondence commences on matters already thought to have been decided and others not yet agreed upon. In between, just before the Christmas of 1672, a letter from Ham tells Bruce how much Lauderdale likes his new Surrey home, 'especially seeing the privacy of itt enables me to write to friends, and to reflect upon their kindness, which I shall never forgett.'

A master joiner was sent up from Ham at this time with the Duke of Lauderdale's commendation. 'I hope you will find satisfaction to employ him in the king's worke.' This is the only reference to any public work in the correspondence for 1672, though we know that Holyrood was in the process of rebuilding throughout the year, and repairs were being done at Stirling and the Bass Rock, and no doubt at other places as well. In fact, between the signing of the Contract in March of 1672, and a short note about repairing the Lord Chancellor's lodgings and the Duke of Hamilton's, there is a curious silence regarding what the King's Architect was doing for his royal and official employer, though his activities in a private capacity, principally for the Duke of Lauderdale, are amply recorded.

I suppose it would be unkind to label the Duke of Lauderdale 'an old woman' (using modern slang), but there is just a hint of it surely in his 'goings-on' about broom cupboards and the kitchen quarters. One would have thought the Duchess could have managed to cope with that sort of thing; but no doubt having got what she wanted by marrying a member of the all-powerful CABAL (literally the tail that wagged the dog in John Maitland's case), she occupied herself mainly with personal agrandisement and the cultivation of Court society. The gorgeous, if often quite vulgar interiors at Ham, begun about 1673 and carried on over some five years, would appear to confirm her disinterestedness in mundane details of running a house, though she dictated what should be done in other spheres *ad nauseum*. It looks as if her husband, bereft of any real personal power, turned to the contemplation, though not always the fulfilment of distant schemes as some relief from the wiles of Bessie and concerned himself again for a while with his old Scottish friends and private Scottish matters, leaving the 'meat' to the Duchess. At any rate as 1673 opens he is back writing in considerable detail to Sir William Bruce about Brunstane, and also Thirlestane, which was not finished even then, and where Bruce was to build at the Duke's expense a delightful Parish Kirk, his only wholly ecclesiastical design and one which might have served as an excellent model for his country, if only there could have been religious peace for any length of time.

Besides sending up a joiner for the 'king's worke' Lauderdale recommends Bruce to employ this man's son at Lawther. This is the first reference to Lawther, or Lauder Kirk, which serves the small burgh of the same name and stands at the gates of Thirlestane Castle (one of Slezer's prints refers to Lauder, not Thirlestane castle). 'I shall send upon bords a patern of the worke for the painter,' the Duke goes on, 'but I think you shall do well to make use of a Dutchman, for there are none here who does worke so well as those of that nation. I beseech you assur your lady of my most affectionate kindness, and be so well as to believe I am your real friend. LAUDERDALE.'

It is a pity, but inevitable, that the bulk of the letters available for research are to rather than from Sir William Bruce, for quite naturally he and Robert Mylne kept the correspondence that came to them, especially from the Duke of Lauderdale; while Lauderdale himself would hardly bother to keep every little note from Bruce or Mylne. It is a pity, however, because a clearer picture of the famous architect might have emerged. As it is Lauderdale completely hogs the scene, his personality popping out of every line he writes. Indeed his letters seem to give an even better indication of his character than his actions, apparently disproving the adage about actions speaking louder than words! It all depends who is behind the actions. Bruce, we know from his recorded behaviour and from his restrained and patrician architecture, was a balanced and dutiful man, a gentleman, in fact, but we rarely in the official documents feel any of his warmth, touch much of the real, live Bruce. References to going down to Thirlestane 'with Wil Bruce' tell us he was likeable, for Christian names were not bandied about in the seventeenth century in the way they are today; but whereas the Duke of Lauderdale is always so anxious to impress upon Sir William Bruce the genuineness of his feelings towards him, in reply to Lauderdale's 'be so well to me to believe I am your real friend etc.' Bruce remains polite and diffident as befits an employee, however well born. The best he can muster is the formal 'Command my Lord, your Lordship's most faithful humble, and obleaged servant.'

Once the correspondence had been taken up again, after nearly a year's silence (following Lauderdale's marriage to the Countess of Dysart), there was no stopping the flow, and what concerned the building of Brunstane, Thirlestane, Lauder Kirk and various alterations at Lethington, occupied page after page of letter space between Sir William Bruce 'att Edinburgh,' and the Duke of Lauderdale; sometimes from Ham, but occasionally from Whitehall. On christmas Eve 1672, for instance, the Duke could not restrain himself from writing to Bruce to say that at last he had definitely decided to build Brunstane next year, 'and therefore I pray you let me have your advice speedily, to the end I may send my positive instructions . . . one thing I am positive in putting my great chamber on the east side facing the sea . . . I much desire a low dining room, and I have designed it as my little low-library. I am not troubled with the narrowness (it is as broad as the galleries at Whitehall) . . . Do not make more haste than you can conveniently with the draught of my other houses, though I would faine have them, especially Thirlstan Castle, for I cannot find them here. And so adieu.'

After Christmas more Brunstane details came to Sir William Bruce's address from 'my Lord,' at Whitehall. Unfortunately, Bruce's in-between letter is not extant, but it evidently enquired of his powerful client if he was satisfied with the drawings for Brunstane,

27 Robert Mylne,
King's Master Mason.
Engraving from
*Master Masons of the
Crown of Scotland*

28 Holyroodhouse, the main elevation as designed
by Bruce and completed in 1679

29 Detail entrance portico showing Royal Coat of Arms as drawn by De Wett and made by Robert Mylne

30 Section through courtyard at Holyrood. From *Master Masons*

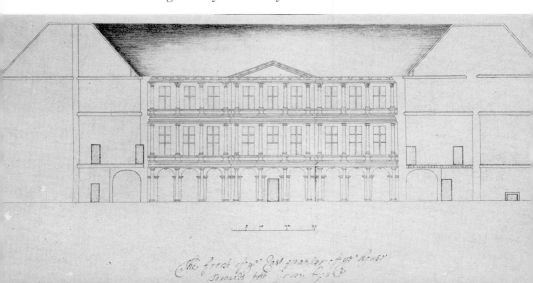

31　Bruce's Courtyard in the style of the Gaston d'Orleans wing at Blois

32　Fretwork ceiling in room intended as Charles II's bedchamber. The decorative features were applied on the spot by craftsmen lying on their backs on scaffolding

33 Grand Staircase. Note traditional Scotch bowtel nosings and returns

34 Part of Long Gallery with portraits by De Wett

35 The Music Room showing typical carving around chimneypiece

6 James, Duke of Albany
and York. Engraving by
Cornelius van Dalen

The Abbey Kirk,
Holyroodhouse. Interior as
appeared in 1688. From
R. Adam's *Vitruvius
Scoticus*

38   Bedroom in Prestonfield House showing 17th century décor

39   The main facade a[s] rebuilt in 1682. Porc[h] moder[n]

40 Wrought-iron stair rail at Caroline Park, near Edinburgh, similar to one installed by Bruce at Craigiehall

41 Gate piers at original (sea) entrance. Note resemblance to piers at Kinross and Marriage Column at Panmure

42 Northern facade at Caroline Park, circa 1685

43 Prospect of Dunkeld from *Theatrum Scotiae*,
showing Dunkeld House (now demolished) centre

44 Court facade, Leslie House (Rothes Palace),
from *Vitruvius Scoticus*

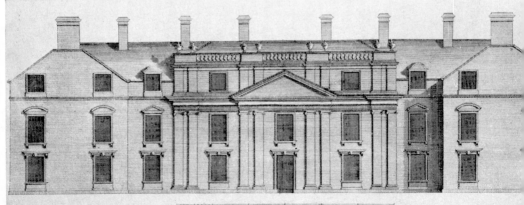

for he is informed; 'I am sure I told you before I was well pleased with the last edition of Brunstein, which I confess was much mended from that I sent down.' Then comes the sting in the tail. 'But there is a necessity of a new addition which I now propose!' The reader will scarcely credit what the Duke does propose, at least not while seriously bearing in mind his somewhat erratic and not altogether blameless career. It is no less than the absolute necessity of a chapel for Brunstane. In a curious sort of way Lauderdale was a religious man, he had been sternly brought up, he was, I suppose, an episcopalian-pagan, as opposed to the King who was, in secret at any rate, a papist-pagan, but he could never quite throw off the influence of his Covenanting days.

It was in pursuance of his quaintly persistent attachment to some form of religion, while at the same time doing precisely what he liked irrespective of the teachings of that religion, that the Duke of Lauderdale insisted on due and adequate provision being made at Brunstane for himself, his wife and the servants to worship God. 'In noe place is a Chapell more necessary than there,' he wrote to Sir William Bruce, 'where the house is so farr from the church, yet my wife and I were pusled where to place it; but at last we condescended on a place.' There were to be two new pavilions on either side of the entrance one of which was to be adapted as a Chapel, 'the servants may enter below, at the foote of the great staire, and there may be convenience above for my wife and me to enter into a loft . . . as for the other new pavilion . . . there will be uses enough for it, and there may be a vault under it.'

This loft was surely a smaller version of the one proposed for the King in the Abbey Kirk at Holyrood, an opera box to all intents and purposes, richly carved and ornamented at the back of the church, high above the congregation, and similar to the one Bruce later erected for the first Earl of Hopetoun at the east end of the Parish Church at Abercorn, of which more anon (it was Bruce's last completed design, and dates from 1708, two years before his death). The Brunstane laird's loft, or gallery, has disappeared, though the pavilion it was in is still there, as are the vaults under the other pavilion (they are now called dungeons and said to have housed wounded prisoners from the Battle of Pinkie Heugh which took place more than a century before that part of the house was built!) Lauderdale thought his pavilions would improve the look of his new 'villa' considerably, and was so keen to see what Bruce would produce in the way of drawings that all he asked for was a rough sketch, 'and upon my approving them you may doe them over againe fairly.' The subject then turns to Thirlestane Castle and the church at Lauder; 'the sooner the church will be removed (the old one) it will be the better. Advertise me what they are doing there, for I have agreed with two Dutchmen who are excellent joiners, and have made all my shapes and lyneings of my rooms at Ham, to goe down, and it may be they will carry with them a Dutch painter with paterns.' This artist must have been the man responsible for the inset panels in the octagonal room at Brunstane, and some panels at Holyrood.

De Wett is also said to have worked first at Ham, though there is only one picture of his there now and the guide book makes the odd comment that he was supposed to have been a pupil of Rubens. 'A pupil of Rubens' in those days cannot have meant what we today would think, but merely someone who studied the works of Rubens *in situ*. Jacob de Wett was by no means a good painter, and if he was 'a pupil of Rubens' (or Rembrandt) the fact is not very obviously reflected in his repetitive official portraits, though he often made a better job of panels and ceilings.

A letter dated 15th April 1673, is full of Lauderdale's new instructions and comments, and is, in some respects, one of the most interesting and important of the series. It is also the last in which the writer's own personal building schemes take precedence over the King's, at Holyrood. After thanking Sir William Bruce for 'the planes and perspectives of my three houses' (Brunstane, Thirlestane and Lethington) he announces he will now give a clear answer to all. 'I am glad the avenue is so hard and it is planted, and that the tarras and the new stairs look so very well; but I am sure the maison work will not be so soon finished. For you may remember that I was very positive to have the two pavilions next the house [these comments are about Thirlestane, not Brunstane], raised one story higher . . . Therefore, without further debate, you shall order the present taking down of the roofs of these two pavilions, and the raising each of them one storey higher, so the same roof will serve again and the same skilly [skailyie, or slates, which at that time literally did resemble skails, with rounded edges at the bottoms], very near. This I know will cost money, but without it I shall never endure the front of my house, and therefore of necessity it must presently be done.'

Instructions about the church at Lawther (Lauder) follow, the Duke saying that his private chapel can be used while the new Parish Kirk is 'abuilding'. 'I do appoynt the carrying away of the old church into the place where the new church is to be built, and that as soon as my chappel may be provided for the parish . . . as for the new church I would have it decent and large enough, with a handsome little steeple, if any of the timber of the old church will serve, it will be cheaper etc.' This delightful village church is cruciform in plan, and has, as Lauderdale wished, a handsome little steeple, octagonal, rising from arches above the central space. It clearly owes something to the similarly cruciform and plainish classical church of Francois Mansart at Balleroy, with which château Thirlestane itself has architectural links. The interior has been altered since Bruce's day for presbyterian worship, and filled with many galleries. In the mid-seventeenth century however, it would have had, as the Lauderdale Chapel at Ham had, a small, squarish Holy Table at the east end, with a red velvet cloth and gold fringe, and candlesticks upon it. No cross, but a velvet cushion for a large Prayer book, or Bible, and on suitable occasions fine plate would be displayed behind. One says this with authority, since what is today on view at Ham House chapel is precisely what was there in 1673.

Bruce's cruciform kirk at Lauder has one or two imitations in other parts of Scotland, at least the tower may be seen in duplicate in Falkirk, but more surprisingly, and significantly the style spread to North America, or so I am told by Dr. Gowans of the Department of Fine Art at Delaware University who is studying the subject. Dr. Gowans has been trying to follow up and trace various Scottish influences in America, the more expected ones in Nova Scotia the less expected further south, in Virginia, a supposedly 'English' preserve. Not so, apparently, for, as a result of persecution and uncertainty during the latter days of Stewart rule, and afterwards, a number of Scottish episcopalian clergy emigrated to the North American Colonies, where, although they administered to a predominantly 'English' biased society, Scoticisms were introduced, including Scottish architecture. Thus, Sir William Bruce's charming Parish Kirk at Lauder, with its ocatgonal steeple over the crossing and cruciform plan, has 'children' across the Atlantic, children raised by exiled Scots ministers pining for Caledonia 'stern and wild' amongst the 'Sassenachs' of Virginia.

After dealing with Lauder Kirk the solicitous laird returns to Brunstane, passing Lethington in the process. Poor old Lethington, ancient east coast stronghold of the Maitlands, erstwhile retreat of Mary, Queen of Scots Secretary of State, it never seems to have been rebuilt properly, what with Brunstane, Thirlestane and Ham, not to mention Lauder Kirk and Holyroodhouse going on the whole time. 'I shall pass by Ledington as you doe,' declares Lauderdale to Bruce. It is pretty certain, however, that some work was done there between 1674 and 1679 when James Duke of York, at the beginning of his technical exile for refusing to subscribe to the Test Act, stopped there and was entertained by the Duke and Duchess of Lauderdale. It was on this occasion that James is reported to have remarked on the dearth of emparked estates in Scotland, and to have caused Lethington to be enclosed by a stone dyke thereby, but I do not think this account of Royal condescension can really be true, since the contract for building the park wall there is dated 1674. The Lethington emparkment may, on the other hand, be the first private one effected in the north.

Lauderdale was pleased with progress at Brunstane but asks Bruce temporarily to soft-pedal plans for the two new pavilions he was so keen on previously. 'As for the sclaiting of the old house, it must be done with blew skailyie as the new . . . and I am very well pleased you are so forward in the preparation for the building, which I pray you let go on.' Some slowing down at Thirlestane is also enjoined so far as extra pavilions are concerned. 'We shall have to do so much raising the western pavilions, and building the church, and making the gardens on the south side, that I will not be guilty of undertaking more for this summer.' The two extra pavilions to which Lauderdale refers, extended beyond the ones he wanted raised, were not in the end built though they appear in the Slezer print. It would seem, therefore, that the enterprising Captain of Artillery obtained copies of Bruce's original plans, and did not wait to see exactly what part of them was finally achieved. At any rate, the Thirlestane Castle project is very thoroughly covered in his *Theatrum Scotiae*, wherein there are two fine birds' eye views and the complete plans. The whole effect as shown is of a Scottish Ham, neat and tidy, the entrance approached between the two outer pavilions (not built), via dignified and beautifully proportioned ceremonial steps to a paved court (chequerboard pattern), with the taller pavilions (the ones whose roofs were eventually raised) on either side. The front door is depicted as it was actually constructed in red sandstone, and in the Doric order, but Slezer's drawing omits what is, in effect, the most dramatic and exciting bit of the entire design, Bruce's huge central tower capped with its immense and suggestive ogee roof. The King's Architect rarely let himself go in this manner, being content on most occasions to let nature provide the drama and to design and set his buildings to be complementary to their surrondings rather than in competition with them. Here however, he has pulled off a grand architectural gesture which presages the modern, so-called Scotch Baronial style. A baronial style in which the assymetrical and varied elements of an earlier' warlike age' defensive towers and turrets, supported by corbelled arches and standing at a great height from the ground, are formalised and made symmetrical to suit the more sophisticated tastes of a period in which architecture even if it still sometimes still looked a little offensive, was only martial in jest.

In the eighteenth century one of the Duke of Lauderdale's descendants employed Robert Adam to draw up plans for a further transformation of Thirlestane. It was probably a good thing these never materialised; but in the next century David Bryce was able to enlarge the house without seriously changing Sir William Bruce's original conception. Bryce was one of those able architects who lived during the period of the 'Battle of the Styles,' in which lovers of re-creative gothic and the devotees of neo-classicism fought for supremacy in art. He practised in both styles, no doubt he had to, but excelled in Baronial recreations. His work at Thirlestane was almost all done in the Bruce manner. True he added a few more turrets than were absolutely necessary, and almost spoiled Lauderdale's pavilions with the roofs raised by sticking out a pair of oriel windows, but in general his work is acceptable. It is also interesting to note that Bryce, himself the arch-priest of Scotch Baronial, recognised his debt to Bruce's experiments of two hundred years earlier not only in the respect he showed for his work at Thirlestane but in the sincerest form of flattery itself, by repeating Bruce's tricks in his own buildings. The re-baronialising of Blair Castle, for instance, refaced for a latter day Duke of Atholl, has a distinct feel of Thirlestane about it.

The interior of Thirlestane owes much less to Bruce, and much more to the Lauderdales, particularly the Duchess, than the exterior, and some of the gorgeous fretwork ceilings are finer even than those at Ham; they are, really, a bit overdone, though in keeping with the sumptuous vulgarity of the Restoration Court. One appreciates this especially when comparing Bruce's own fretwork ceilings at Balcaskie, and at Kinross, and the better examples at Holyrood. They were all the work of either or both George Dunsterfield and John Halbert, Charles II's favourite plasterers. There is something about Thirlestane, and Ham, that places the Lauderdales in the Fouquet class of builders and decorators. They wished to shine above the King, and they seem to have managed to do so without incurring Charles II's envy or wrath, or suffering the kind of retaliation inflicted on Fouquet by Louis XIV. At Vaux-le-Vicomte the famous French financier overstretched himself, he was dismissed and imprisoned; and his audacity provoked the King into building Versailles, so big and so magnificent that no mere subject could possibly compete.

By the summer of 1673 all talk of Thirlestane is dropped, and the repairs and rebuilding at Holyrood take precedence for the next four or five years. Evidently progress at Thirlestane had been such by then that the various craftsmen sent up by Lauderdale could be spared for the King's work. They included, besides the celebrated plasterers before-mentioned, a number of Dutchmen, mostly stone masons and carvers, and Dutch painters. I do not think the 'Germanes' to whom Lauderdale refers in his last letter on Thirlestane went on to Holyrood, their style is quite distinctive and altogether heavier and less pure in detail than anything in the rebuilt palace. 'They have wrought much for the finishing of this House [Ham],' writes the Duke in the spring of 1673, 'and have made the double chassee for the windows.' This is a reference to the partial installation of sash windows at Ham, the older, Jacobean rooms being yet supplied with opening-out casements, the newer with sliding sashes. This is how Holyrood was fitted until restored for the visit of George IV in 1822. The windows in the old Stewart tower, with their casements and leaded lights, were repeated by Bruce in his balancing tower, while at the back sliding sashes with wooden astragals were fitted. This is plainly visible in old prints and is similar to what was done at Brunstane.

The 'Germanes,' according to Lauderdale, 'are sober fellows, understand English enough, and most excellent workmen, both at that trade (joinery), and for the making of cabinets. Within these ten days they will be readay, and shall bring with them full instructions concerning the finishing both of Thirlestane Castle and Brunstein. They shall also bring with them paterns for hinges and bolts . . . I shall send them by sea to New Castle, where John Cockburn shall dispatch them to Thirlestane Castle by land . . . I shall say no more but that I am your real friend to serve you. LAUDERDALE.' I do not think this means that the 'Germanes' did the octagonal room at Brunstane, with its original sash windows, as both finish and design are modest, restrained and refined compared to contemporary work at Thirlestane, where the state ante-room is clearly the work of central and not northern European craftsmen. Indeed the ante-room in question is probably the only thing left by these 'two excellent joyners' (Lauderdale's 'Germanes'), north of the border, and thus stands in a class on its own. There is nothing either at Brunstane or Holyrood in the same *genre*, nor is this particular work even typical of Restoration taste as a whole in the Britain of Charles II. We are here in fancy in the hall of a foreign prince, somewhere east of the Rhine, possibly south of Heidelberg, faced with an ostentatious bowlderisation of Palladian detail relieved by quaint Michelangelesque touches. [4] Taken with the deeply set and extraordinarily ornate fretwork ceiling above, the total design would not disgrace a film set for a Ruritanian romance. Such a display of wealth and pretention scarcely has any equal in its period in the United Kingdom, except possibly in the north drawing room at Ham House, likewise created to gratify the notoriously vain John Maitland and the exacting Eliza Murray, Duke and Duchess of Lauderdale.

[1] Jacobite sympathizers were later sent to the Bass, but not poor Sir William Bruce, the Castles of Edinburgh and Stirling being considered safe enough in his case.

² Mackenzie features in Evelyn's *Diary* several times, he is said to have held the theory that Presbyterianism was introduced into Scotland by a Jesuit priest in order to seduce the people. If so he seems to have succeeded.

³ I have this from the late Hamilton More Nisbet, architect and proprietor of 'The Drum,' who told me he had the original bills.

⁴ Perhaps only in the Portugal of Dom Joao V, where German architects and craftsmen were employed almost contemporaneously, does one find the same romantic feeling, far from its Central European source.

Holyroodhouse in the late 17th century

CHAPTER FIVE

Holyrood completed

WE HAVE SEEN how the original idea for the rehabilitation of the Royal Palace of Holyroodhouse was to restore the damage done during the Cromwellian occupation and to complete the whole palace as intended by King Charles I, and designed for him by his Master Mason and Captain of the Pioneers, John Mylne. This design was, in essence, an extended and classicised implementation of an older scheme approved a century earlier in the reign of James IV, which unfortunately, never quite got 'off the ground.' At first Sir William Bruce's instructions were based on fulfilling 'his Majesties deare fathere's intentione,' but this proved too expensive, and in the event not really necessary for a King who, if he proposed to come to Scotland at all, had no desire to linger long in his northern Kingdom. Charles II had suffered untold misery there in his youth, when, in the hands of the Covenanters, he had been made to sign documents the contents of which he abhorred, and to listen to harangues and arguments the tenor of which would have tried the patience of a saint, let alone the future 'Merry Monarch.'

As it happened there was not immediately available enough money to restitute or carry out everything Charles I intended, and Bruce, while maintaining the same general form as John Mylne had drawn out, was forced to reduce and curtail certain features in order that his royal patron could more easily cut his coat according to his cloth. Thus he proposed only one internal courtyard instead of two, no elongation of the west front as shown on Mylne's approved plans, and the existing turreted entrance between the old James IV towers and the new Charles II one was to remain, though it was out of keeping with Bruce's classical concept. Between 1671 and 1673 work on this amended scheme proceeded unabated. The Bishop and Dean of Edinburgh, and others with 'rights' and parcels of property at Holyrood, were bought out wherever possible and provided with alternative accommodation; and by August 1673 the bulk of the rebuilt palace was well above ground and quite a lot of it actually finished. The parts burned down in 1650 by negligent Roundhead troops had all been restored and orders were given for Bruce to make ready the lodgings apportioned to the Lord Chancellor (The Earl of Rothes), and the Hereditary Keeper of the Palace (The Duke of Hamilton). [1]

By the end of 1674 it became clear that there was, after all, going to be more money available than was at first thought, and a further Royal Warrant was made towards the work at Holyroodhouse. A report on progress made on December 19th, 1674, by Lauderdale's brother, Charles Maitland, Lord Hatton, who at this stage was Treasurer Depute to the King and rising rapidly in favour, is interesting in its details. From it one can see that the 'bones' of the present Palace were already there, 'the great gallerie whollie finished in rooff floorings, plastering, timber linings, windows, casements, glass, doors, locks, Ironwork in all the stories thereoff Excepting only some few finishing above the doors and chimneys . . . The East Quarter [the present Royal Apartments], Is wholly finished except the ground storie, All the windows in cases and casements finished.' No mention is made of 'chassie' or sash windows, they were all latticed casements then, glazed, as itemised bills show, 'in french glass of the best. The King's great Bed chamber [now the music room], and Ante chamber Are farr advanced in the plaster being fyne fretwork.' The ceiling in what was planned as King Charles II's bedroom, but in which he never slept, is probably the most magnificent and daring of Halbert and Dunsterfield's plaster masterpieces. The oval central panel contains a quite good painting by De Wett, and the whole elaborate ceiling was meant to be touched up with gold and other bright colours to create an impression of sensuous luxury in imitation of Italian palaces.

The new tower was finished in 1674, so far as the masonwork was concerned. 'The timber rooff thereof is finished and ready to put on. All the casses of the windows in the South [new], quarter and tower ready. . . none of that quarter nor of the new tower Is yet floored, but the flooring daills [boards], Are all readie to lay down and seasoned and waits only for the putting on of the rooff.' Vast quantities of building materials had been assembled for the work over the preceding three years, while the timber had been seasoning, 'And it is Judged by all that the provision of daills will be sufficient to finish the whole house in floorings, divisiones, doors, plastering, and sarking of the roof.' Nothing seems to have been left out, neither 'oyll,' nor 'whyt lead for common painting of the house . . . or sufficient provisions of marble stones and tyles for chimneys.' Many of these will have been fetched or bought abroad by Bruce on his trips to Holland and France, where he was able to establish commercial contacts for such things and have them dispatched by sea in quantity enough to supply not only the Royal wants but Lauderdale's and his own. The Royal Treasurer Depute did, however, find a few items wanting. 'Of marble chimneys for the 2nd. storie Ther is wanting 10. Locks and Keyes are wanting for the East and South quarters, Ther is no nails in store.'

There still seems to have been some difficulty in buying up awkward bits of land in the vicinity, for another item mentioned by Lord Hatton concerns the necessity 'to agree for a piece of ground to be ane entrie to the Church so that the present passage may be stopt which Incommods the north syde of the north quarter exceedingly and a small charge will doe it.' This refers to the tiny space behind the Commendator's House and the Long Gallery; and judging by contemporary prints the Lords in Council were not able to do much about it, for the sixteenth century house, two storeyed and with high pitched roof and dormers, continued to rise awkwardly on the site adjacent to the original Stewart tower of the palace, effectively blocking the entrance to the Church at ground level. The Royal pew in its elaborate box, was of course above, and entered from the far end of the Long Gallery through an opening now permanently closed.

The sudden rise in favour of Lord Hatton, Lauderdale's brother, can be explained in two ways. First and foremost his sedulous cultivation of the powers-that-be, and his fairly thorough carrying out of his commission; but more importantly by the fact that he was the Duke of Lauderdale's heir, since neither by Anne Home nor the Countess of Dysart did John Maitland have a son, so that his Dukedom became extinct when he died in 1682. His former Earldom went to Lord Hatton, the King's Treasurer-Depute, who had already been made (in 1678), Surveyor of the Palace of Holyroodhouse in place of the gentlemanly Sir William Bruce. The Treasurer-Depute was granted apartments in Holyrood, in a Royal Warrant, dated March 9th, 1675, and signed by his brother. 'Whereas We have seen fit that the Lord Hatton, our Treasurer Deput be Lodged in our Palace of Holyrood House for his better accommodation in his constant attendance upon our Service . . . Therefore our will and pleasure is, and we do hereby require you forthwith to give order that these Lodgings be put in sufficient repair etc. . . By His Majesties Command.'

Work went on steadily throughout 1675 until December, when it appears the water supply dried up and an urgent letter was sent by the Lords Commissioners to Sir William Bruce asking him to search for new sources. 'The spring water of St. Antons [St. Anthony's Well, a spring of some antiquity in the King's Park at Holyrood, on a spot now marked by the folly ruin known as St. Anthony's Chapel], is failed and dried up and albeit it shoulde returne againe will not be sufficient to serve all the ludgeings within the Palace. You are therefore hereby ordered to search for other springs within the Park of Holyroodhouse or any place elsewhere . . . and convey them in to such places as those who ludge therein may be conveniently accommodated and provided with watter.' I wonder what present day architect would be able to comply with such orders? Bruce had to be a 'jack of all trades,' a real architect not just the man who added the decoration; a man such as Vitruvius described, who knew everything, controlled everything, and did not leave the mathematical and constructional details to an engineer, or the surveying to a land expert. He found the water, and also designed Edinburgh's regular waterworks. *Extracts from the Records of the Burgh of Edinburgh, 1665 to 1680,* show that the Town Council sought Sir William Bruce's advice as early as 1672 for their project of bringing water (the first piped supply), to the Town; and the works were subsequently carried out to his design.

There is one thing to be said in Lord Hatton's favour, he usually saw that the architect, masons and other contractors were properly paid, and there seems to have been no undue pressure brought to bear on him or the authorities in order to achieve this very satisfactory and not very common situation (I speak as an architect). In fact, a full account of what had been spent and what was owed, (coming to a total of '£52490 Scots,' or 'four thousand three hundred and seaventy-four pounds, three shillings and four pence sterline money'), was drawn up in Edinburgh on February 15th, 1676 and agreed by Charles II a week later. 'Wee have seen and considered yours of the 15th instant . . . And wee doe approve of the totall Summe mentioned in your estimate . . . for the arreares of workman, and fees and salaries due for worke done before the first day of this instant; as also for levelling the Gardens, Gravell and Grasseworks and bringing in water to the House.' The King asks that special care may be taken to see that the money paid for materials for the rebuilding of the palace is used to best advantage, 'both as to cheapnes and usefulness . . . and that you will find any unnecessary Fees or Salareies you will cut them off.' In the same warrant Charles II decides to remove the whole of the existing connecting entrance wing between the two towers; and a month later another Royal Warrant is sent up to Sir William Bruce to rebuild the entrance in the Classical Orders.

Charles II exhibited that consideration for others which distinguished his race down the centuries, he possessed to a remarkable degree that royal condescension and memory for faces and facts that is the hall mark of true royalty, so that when he heard that Robert

Mylne, his Master-mason, had suffered losses in the work at Holyrood he authorised his 'right trusty and wellbeloved Cousins and Councellors, the Lords Commissioners of our Treasury of our ancient Kingdome of Scotland,' to give him the Summe of five hundred pounds sterline money besides what is condition to be payed unto him by the contract.' There followed a warrant, dated 'Edinburgh last of February 1676,' from the Lords Commissioners to Sir William Bruce to take down the buildings erected by the 'usurpers,' and 'to designe and order the rebuilding thereof in pillar work conforme to and with the Dorick and Ionick Orders and to finish the ends above . . . with the Corinthien style.' A meeting was arranged between Lord Hatton, Bruce and Robert Mylne to settle exactly what was to be done, to fix a date for completing the work that had already been begun, and to agree plans in duplicate for the proposed new work. Sir William is also 'to bring off of the watter that comes from St. Anthonies well a branch or small pipe of about halfe inch bore with that watter pure and unmixed with any other that comes directly from that spring to be setled to run out at the most convenient place he can contrive for publick use, and that the whole other work beside the Mason worke be finished within 12 moneths efter the date hereof.'

Two new Contracts were made 'betwixt Sir Wm. Bruce of Balcaskie knight and baronett His Majestie's Surveyare Generall and Sir William Sharp of Stainiehill knight his Majesties Cash Keeper *on the ane pairt* and Robert Mylne His Majesties Master Meassone *on the ither pairt.*' The first, dated March 1676, was for £3888 Scots about (£320 sterling), and concerned the 'taking down of Ashlar Work and Rought Work within on the West Quarter built by the English [Cromwell] at His Majesties Palace of Holyrood.' The second, the most important and the one that resulted in the present handsome entrance with its pillared gateway, beautifully sculptured Royal Coat of Arms and Imperial Crown above being constructed, is dated July 1676 and is for the sum of £4200 Scots (roughly £350 sterling). The wording is very precise and worth repetition, I think, if only on account of the quaint architectural terminology. After binding Robert Mylne to take down the front wall of the palace 'from the Battlemente to the Bottome And to rebuild upon the old fundatione in exact aisler [ashlar], smoothe as paiper close joynted,' he is instructed, 'to make ane gaitt of the Dorricke order Tuo columnes upon each syde of the said gaitt with pedeestell Basse colume chapterhead [capital], and intablator [entablature], of ane Modell according to threttie ane foott height Raill and Ballesters and pilasters with finisheing above about and alongest the said intablitowre (they certainly varied their spelling and knew not punctuation!), quich rownes from towre to towre As also above the cornishe [cornice] of the In syde to the quholl breadth of the court. The cornishe enriched onelie with dentellei [a dental course].' There follows further details as to doors, architraves and so on, and then a reference to the Coat of Arms, 'the Scotts armes is to be sett exactlie weill cut with the supporters standing on the said plint [plinth], Mantleing crowne & cresit built and wrought weill in ane handsome copairtment or howseing . . . as the same quholl worke is particularlie designed extenditt and seigned by the said Surveyar (Sir Wm. Bruce).'

This Coat of Arms is especially interesting as it shows the Lion Rampant shield within the collar of the Most Noble and Ancient Order of the Thistle, an order which was founded by James III in the fifteenth century but which never had precise rules drawn up for it and which today is governed by the Constitution given by Charles II's brother, James, when as king he revived the Order as a meaningful entity and caused the Abbey Kirk at Holyrood to be re-edified as the Chapel of that Order. This was in 1687, the last year of his disastrous reign, I will return to it later. The 1676 contracts are particularly precise too on the subject of payment and the dire consequences to the Master Mason should any of his work prove faulty, in which case it would have to be taken down and rebuilt (at his expense). The exact amount to be paid to Mr Mylne for materials is mentioned and an allowance made for old stone from the demolished portion. The most modern practice of withholding part payment until some time after the completion of the work by the masons is incorporated in this splendid document, which in every respect is as tight, and yet sensible, as any twentieth century counterpart and would comply, I am sure, with all the requirements of the Professional Code of Practice of the Royal Institute of British Architects.

The July Contract between Bruce, Sharp and Mylne is the last of the important documents concerned with the rebuilding of Holyrood, though there are very many bills and notes in respect of minor matters, park walls, garden paths, taking down what were virtually sheds in front of the palace, repairing windows, replacing damaged materials; and these applied to Stirling Castle and other Royal Properties in Scotland for which the King's Architect and Master Mason had responsibility. Besides these the actual Account Book of the Expenses incurred in repairing the Royal Palaces and Castles in Scotland is extant, being deposited in the Register House in Edinburgh after its discovery intact in the Charter Chest at Kinross House in the nineteenth century. It would be tedious to go through the entire list of payments here, and I feel in any case that I have probably quoted quite enough from the letters already, but a number of items are of peculiar interest and definitely worth mentioning, such as the payment of £98. 12. of Scots money 'to Jacob de Wett — Dutch Paynter — for two several chimney pieces paynted by him and for paynting in marble coullour ane chimney . . . £252 to John Halbert and George Dunserfield, Inglish plaisterers . . . for plaistering the 3rd roome in the 3rd storie of the inner syde of the north quarter of this Pallace measuring in all with the cornice 70 yards.' This was in 1674, the same year in which George Dunsterfield (the 't' seems to have been optional) worked at Balcaskie for Bruce at 3s. 6d. per day.

Nearly £1000 Scots is paid to Robert Mylne for wages due to masons and barrowmen, and the sum of £774. 13. 'to Allex Eizatt, Plumber for casting, working and laying upon the roofe of this Palace 2323 stones 14½ lb. weyt of lead.' He was one of the several Eizats employed by Bruce at different times and in different places, including William Eizat, who did the carving and wrightwork at Abercorn in 1707/8, and another Alexander, who in 1688 took the sizes of the timber for the inside finishings at Kinross to be brought from Holland. Item 23 in the 1674 Account is 'By maintenance of the Cart Horse (that is keept for carrying away the rubbish of this Palace at 12s. Scots each day from Sept. 1. 1673 to March 1 instant being 181 days, £108. 12. 0.' On August 3rd 1674, 'The accomptants Sallarie [£2700], for the space of three qrters preceding this instant term of Lammas,' was paid to the 'Generall Surveyer of his Majesties works in this Kingdome.' Other interesting items include the cost of importing 'whyte lead and tylles' from Holland to Leith [only £25], and £1135 Scots claimed by the Glasier 'for the haill Glass work and furnishing, wrought and furnished by him to the said Pallace and horse and foote gaurdes from March 1671 to Nov. 1674.'

The 1675 list shows that both the King's Surveyor and the Cart Horse had become somewhat more expensive to keep, and the horse cost £153. 17s. 'which is more than att any tyme heirtofore placed in respect of the dearth of horse provisiones.' Alexander Eizat the Plumber is mentioned again, and 'Mr. De Wett — Paynter — for ane piece of historie paynted and placed in the roofe of the Kings bedchamber in the second storie of the East qrtr on the syde toeards the privie garden.' received £120. This is the famous central panel in the present music room. John Callender's name appears for the first time in 1676, he was the King's Smith and worked ten years later at Kinross. He was paid £137. 14. for, amongst other things, 'secureing and closing up the windows to keep out the stormie weather the tyme that my Lord Commissioner his Grace was heir' (we know who that was!). On December 15th 1675, John Maisterton, the glazier asked for £211. 10. to cover the cost of supplying '311 footes of new English Glass . . . put by him in the Church of Hallyrudehouse, and for taking doune and putting up agayn in the said church 130 footes of old Glass which said glass windows being repaired, the tyme my Lord Commissioner his Grace was heir for the better accommodation of his Grace . . . which otherwayes would not have been ordered to have been repaired on his Majesties expense.' The final item for 1676 is the large sum of £1564. 2. 6. paid 'to John Houlbert, Plaisterer, for severall sorts of plaistering work wrought by him since his coming to Scotland to work at the said Pallace . . . by him or George Dunsterfield his pairtner.'

The total discharge is given as 'Thriescore fourtein thousand tuo hundred nyntie punds six shillings, 3d. scots' (£6341 Sterling), and signed CH. MAITLAND. While an abstract of the discharge on other works in progress for the King in Scotland (Edinburgh and Stirling Castles and the Bass Rock), taken together with the money paid out to Sir William Bruce for Holyroodhouse, comes to a grand 'summa' of £87,512. 9. 4. Scots. It appears that this amount still left a deficit of around six thousand pounds for Bruce to 'hold compt in his next accompts.' The accounts go on until March 13th. 1679, when a discharge of £102,786 6. 9. (£8565 Sterling) is recorded, and the excess charge had been reduced, (no doubt by Sir William Bruce's careful management), to just over two thousand pounds Scots, which sum was 'instantly delivered unto Sir Wm. Sharp, his Majesties Cash Keeper for his Majesties use,' by the Lords Commissioners, who 'heirby exoner and discharge Sir Wm. Bruce Accomptant of the whole foresaid Charge and of all others soums of money received by him . . . in manner above mentionat for noe and ever.' Bruce was dismissed his post as Surveyor to the King by Lauderdale on May 30th. 1678, on the excuse that the rebuilding of Holyrood was then complete, which of course it was not, though the bulk of the hard work had been done and all that remained was largely a tidying up process and the settling of costs. 'Seeing that Gift [the office of Surveyor Generall], was granted by us to the said Sir William for deseigning and ordering the Buildings and repaireing our Palace of Holyroodhouse & other reparations then commanded by us And that now the said Buildings and reparations are finished and that there is no further use of any such Office of Surveyor Generall Therfor it is our Will and pleasure and wee do hereby declare the said Gift of Surveyour Generall etc. etc. to be voide and null Extincted Expired & recalled by us etc. — By his Majesties command. LAUDERDALE.'

On October 19th of the same year 'CHARLES R', acting again on his Commissioner's advice, appointed Lord Hatton, (his Treasurer

Depute and Lauderdale's brother and heir presumptive), Overseer for the care and reparation of Holyroodhouse and other Royal property in Scotland. 'You are to give all necessary orders thereanent and to employ workmen . . . And particularly our Pallace of Holyroodhouse that the same be finished and compleated in all the buildings Offices Courts Gardens and haill accommodations Avenues and severall pertinents thereof And of our Castles of Edinburgh, Striveling [Stirling], Dumbarton, Blacknesse and our Island of the Basse etc. etc. By his Majesties command. LAUDERDALE.' This was followed on the same day by an order, also from the Duke of Lauderdale, to the Keeper of the Palace (The Duke of Hamilton) to provide him with 'convenient lodgings within our Palace of Holyroodhouse in the South Quarter thereof including the new Tower, Together with Coach house and Stables — By his Majesties command. LAUDERDALE.'

The final accounts for Holyrood are much on the same lines as the previous ones, and although Bruce was officially 'extincted, expired and recalled' in May 1678, he was really responsible, at the end of the day, for the monetary side of things, until exonerated in March 1679. Alexander Eizat, the plumber, is joined by two more of his family, Thomas and another Alexander, the first employed 'setting up nyne marble chimneys,' sent from London at Lauderdale's instigation, the second 'for Upputting severall lyneings of windowes, washing boards, doores, doore pieces, chimneypieces, wall plates and architraves,' for which he was paid £1360 : 19s; a largish amount which suggests he was of some importance. This Alexander was evidently the same wright whom Sir William Bruce later engaged on his own house at Kinross. John Halbert appears again, twice, with big bills for plasterwork; and 'Mr. De Wet — Paynter, for drawing and extending at large his Majesties two coates of Armes with supporters etc. belonging thereto to be a patern to the Meason for cutting the saids coates of armes in stone . . . the one whereof stands since put up upon the middle of the upper pairt of the west fronteice of the east qrtr of the Pallace and the other over the top of the gate [the big Royal Scottish Achievement over the main entrance].'

It is not crystal clear if the 'meason' himself cut the Coat of Arms as part of his job or merely prepared the stones ready for a professional carver. One might have supposed it required an expert to carve this very fine object, but the only reference to such a person is to 'Jan Vansantvoort — Carver, for cutting carving and upputting of several pieces of carved work upon the chimney and door pieces of his Majesties appartment in the east qrtr.' Van Sant Voort, to give the man his separated surname, probably only carved in wood, he did the very fine carving in the Royal Apartments and was employed by

45 Kinross House from the drive

46 The 'gap' showing piers

47   Part Stable Block completed 1686

48   Detail entrance showing cartouche with Arms
of Sir Wm. Bruce and Mary Halket. Note incised
carving in the French manner over modern porch

49 West elevation with gazebo and formal 'court.'
Note attic windows and clever placing of chimney
stalks

50 View showing garden house and back of wing
wall. Note mezzanine windows of mansion

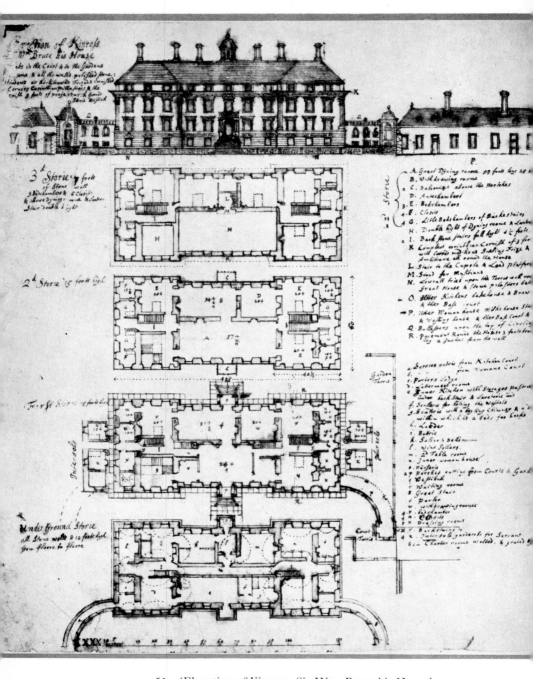

51 'Elevation of Kinross, Sir Wm. Bruce his House'

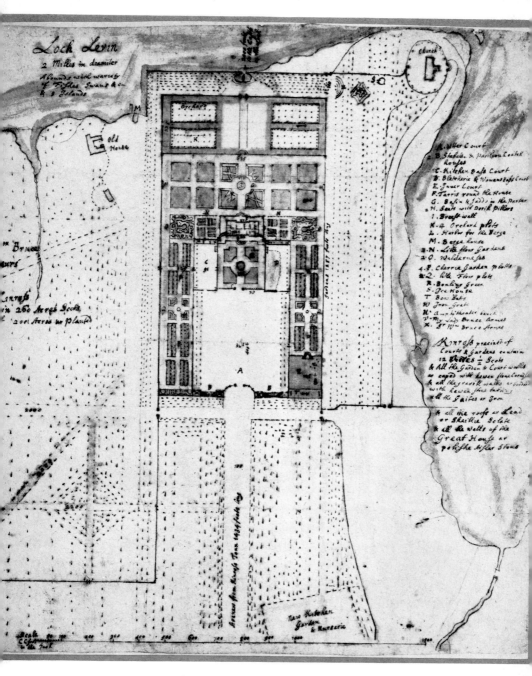

52 Bruce's layout for Kinross. Note Old Manor (left), and Church,
(right) both subsequently demolished

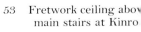

53 Fretwork ceiling above main stairs at Kinro

54 Part stair showing elaborately carved panels

55 Typical corner chimney-piece in what was probably Bruce's 'little tobacco room'

56 Palladian entrance hall in the style of Ashburnham House. Note Jan Sant Voort's carving of Bruce's Arms over doorway, left distance

57 Garden front at Kinross. Note original porch
and wrought-ironwork

58 'Fish gate' with Loch Leven Castle beyond.
Note 'congelations'

Bruce at Prestonfield House, near Edinburgh, when that building was rebuilt after a fire in 1681. For £36 Scots, Van Sant Voort also cut Sir William Bruce's own Coat of Arms, in wood, which is now over the doorway to the cloakroom at the foot of the main stairs at Kinross. He did this in 1679, some years before the building of the house itself was begun, which suggests that Bruce may have made use of Dutch craftsmen whilst they were still available in Edinburgh. Mr Marshall thinks Jan Van Sant Voort probably carved the more intricate parts of the elaborate and beautiful timber staircase panels at Kinross, but if so he could scarcely have done it much earlier that 1690, unless he made the panels separately and someone else fixed them in position later on. There is certainly nothing quite like the Kinross staircase at Holyrood.

Two other Dutchmen, Peter Paul Boyse and Cornelius Van Nerven, were responsible for the best of the stone carving at Kinross, so perhaps they may have had a hand in things at Holyrood, though again, there is really nothing comparable in design and finish at Holyroodhouse, nothing in the whole of Scotland, except possibly at Drumlanrig Castle, to the refined and consummately executed swags and trophies in the Louis XIV style over the front porch at Kinross. These two Dutchmen were paid £600 Scots a year for their labours, 8d. each for their fares to Kinross, 10d. per day for board and lodging in the town, and 2s. 6d. for laundry over a period of three months. The fact that they subsequently worked for the first Duke of Queensberry at Drumlanrig has given rise to the belief that Bruce may have designed that vast pink edifice, the last true Scottish 'chateau,' which is, in fact, a slightly grander version, in the wilds of Dumfriesshire, of Heriot's Hospital in Edinburgh. Personally, I think Robert Mylne himself carved the King's Coat of Arms at Holyrood.[2] He was perfectly capable of bold straightforward work of this kind.

One last item from the Holyrood Accounts is perhaps worth mentioning. Dated March 3rd. 1677, it adds up to the sum of £1217. 18. 0., which when broken up into components is shown thus :

'To sex hundreth fyne large wanscott planks readie sawen, imported from Rotterdam for Lyneing severall of the roomes of the King's owne appartment . . . . £1047. 0. 0.

Payed for Dutie thereof Custome House Leith . . . . . . 42.10. 0.

Freight theerof as per agreement . . . . . . 120. 0. 0.

For entrie and sufferance money . . . . . . 1. 4. 0.

For carieing therof from the Ship to a Closs yaird . . . . 7. 4. 0.

After all this it seems a pity the King never saw what had been so carefully and expensively prepared for him, for although he may not have been enthusiastic about revisiting his northern Kingdom after the Restoration the accommodation provided against such a possibility, and the standard of the design and workmanship, certainly deserved Royal approbation in the flesh. In fact it was the not especially artistic James, Duke of York, who arrived, in the autumn of 1679, cunningly sent to Scotland as the King's Commissioner to save him from the consequences of refusing to take The Test. In his youth this Prince had joined the French army under Turenne in order to avoid his mother's proselytizing and to keep his word to his father, the Martyr King, that on no account would he desert the Anglican Church. Yet after marrying the girl he had seduced in Holland (an act as stupid and distasteful to her father, the future Lord Chancellor Clarendon, as it was annoying to Charles II), he became, like her, a convert to the 'New Religion of Trent.'

Anne Hyde, the Chancellor's daughter, died in 1671 and James afterwards married the pretty Italian Princess Maria Beatrice d'Este, daughter of the Duke of Modena; and since he would not conform to the laws of the protestant establishment, he was exiled, first to Holland, then to Scotland, which, having its own Parliament, technically counted as a foreign country. Nor was the Test so methodically applied as in England, its wording was ambiguous, deliberately so, in order to excuse the friends of the Lords Commissioners and to catch their enemies. The King's brother, therefore, was not likely to find himself in difficulties north of the border, or at least not the same ones as in the south, and in practice his sojourn in Scotland as Charles II's 'Viceroy' was a success from his point of view, and from most other people's.

It was James, Duke of York, who by his dignified and grave manner and sedulous attention to the duties of Lord High Commissioner laid the seeds of that intense loyalty to his house, particularly amongst the Highland Clans, which was to show itself so strongly in 1715, and again to a greater extent still in 1745, and which has since become legendary. His artistic sensibilities may have been limited, though Andrew Fletcher of Saltoun, uncle of the Judge who later lived at Brunstane, found his conversation adequately intellectual; and in any case, his consort made up for James' cultural reserve in some measure. Mary of Modena gave concerts, balls and dinner parties and encouraged amateur dramatics. She is also credited with introducing the tea drinking habit into Scotland. The amateur theatricals at Holyrood included a performance, in honour of Queen Catherine of Braganza's birthday, of Nathaniel Lee's *Mithridates, King of Pontus*, which John Dryden the poet derided from the safe distance of Oxford, though he himself had composed the epilogue. The Catchpel, or real tennis court, also witnessed a revival; James was a keen sportsman, and tennis, not to mention golf on Leith Links, was a favourite pastime during his stay in the north. Much more significantly, however, the Duke-Commissioner demonstrated an unexpected interest in architecture and town-planning which led to his emulating his remoter ancestors in this respect and inaugurating a new era in building and development in Scotland, and Edinburgh in particular.

Sir William Bruce had been dismissed his post as Surveyor General for the rebuilding of Holyrood, which was now occupied by the Ducal Court, but that did not mean his services were not required elsewhere. The Corporation, encouraged by the Duke of York, who granted a charter to the Magistrates and Council giving them the power to extend their 'royalties,' or boundaries, to collect 'cellarage' (taxes levied by the Crown on cellars and areas below the King's Highway) and to erect the necessary 'bridges, arches and new ports,' employed Bruce on their Water Works. Also to complete the tower of Heriot's Hospital, and subsequently to design an Exchange and the first North Bridge. The drawings for the latter, the essential link between the old medieval town of Edinburgh and the proposed newer quarters, were said, by Alexander Kincaid (*History of Edinburgh 1794*), to have been deposited in the Exchequer Court, an institution now merged partly with the Treasury and partly in the Scottish Court of Session. The first North Bridge actually to be built was designed by William Mylne, great-grandson of Robert, the King's Master Mason, by which time the term mason had been exchanged for that of architect, though it cannot be said that William Mylne was substantially more of an architect than his great-grandfather, in whom the occupations of mason and architect were really one. Bruce's status was somewhat different, he was more of a true architect, the designer and supervisor of works, not their constructor. Even William Adam, who is normally vouchsafed the title of architect, was not an architect in the sense Sir William Bruce was, or Inigo Jones, or Wren, or modern architects. Adam both practised as architect and mason (under Sir John Clerk of Penicuik); and made money out of building materials, which would today mean his instant expulsion from the Royal Institute of British Architects!

This is not perhaps the best place to dwell at length on the laying out and building of Edinburgh's famous New Town, the Bicentenary of whose founding in 1767 has just been celebrated, yet, when Lord Provost Drummond laid the foundation stone of William Mylne's North Bridge, he declared; 'We have only begun to fulfil what the Duke (afterwards James VII) first proposed.' Bruce's plans for the bridge seem now to have gone the way of all flesh, neither the City Archivist nor anyone else I have asked can trace them; but it was certainly James, Duke of York, who originated what was eventually done after his time, and which today is the envy not only of other cities in Great Britain but of town-planners and architects all over Europe. Indeed, the New Town of Edinburgh has but few rivals; in France, possibly the eighteenth century quarters of Nancy (built for Stanislas, exiled Polish father-in-law of Louis XV); in Italy, Turin (laid out for Victor Amadeus of Savoy when he acquired the Kingship of Sardinia in 1713); and neo-classic St. Petersburg, begun by Peter the Great and continued throughout two centuries on the same basic plan.[3] Petersburg's long, repetitive terraces and vast open spaces have smaller echoes in Edinburgh squares and crescents, and in Royal and Regent's Terraces, with facades a quarter of a mile long. Nowhere else in Europe is there quite the same extensive use of the neo-classic idiom.

One more echo before we leave the brother of Charles II and his connection with the New Town of Edinburgh. When King James fled abroad, in 1688, he was followed into exile by a number of Scottish gentlemen amongst whom was the Earl of Mar. This Earl developed a great homesickness and a yearning to do something positive for his native land. He was very interested in cultural matters, in later years helping to entertain the 'Old Pretender' (James, Francis Edward, James VII and II's son by Mary of Modena) by organising chamber music concerts and other elevating ways of whiling away the time. Earlier than this, however, he worked assiduously on the ideas his Royal Master had first propounded whilst Lord High Commissioner in Edinburgh between 1679 and 1683, and upon the advancement of which Sir William Bruce had had some influence. The Earl of Mar codified these tentative proposals and composed a thorough report on them, bequeathing the result of his labours to posterity in manuscipt form.[4] Amongst other things he advocated the diverting of the Water of Leith (Edinburgh's 'river') to flow into the Nor' loch and so provide a navigable basin right in the middle of the city; and this was to be linked to the west of Scotland by the Forth and Clyde Canal. The Earl also invented the idea of Prince's Street, on the site of the Lang Gait (or long walk), a footpath then running east to west where the renowned thoroughfare now is. The canal was built, and so was Prince's Street, plus the bridge that Lord Mar, James, Duke of York and Bruce planned, but not the port. It would have been rather a novel type of city with a sea basin at its centre, the view from Prince's Street embracing, besides the view of the castle on its high rock opposite and the line of spires and tall 'lands' running down to Holyrood, cranes and derricks and ships masts and funnels in between.

1 Reference is made in a document of 1674 to the planting of an orchard of pear trees for the Duke of Hamilton's 'ludgings'.

2 Robert Mylne's initials are carved on a pier of the courtyard arcading near the entrance at Holyrood.

3 The Scots architect Charles Cameron may be credited with influencing much of the work done here in the late 18th and early 19th centuries.

4 See, *The Earl of Mar's Legacies to Scotland and to his son Lord Erskine, 1722–1727*, edited from the original M.S. at Alloa House (Scottish History Society).

Detail east gate, Panmure

CHAPTER SIX

After Holyrood

ALTHOUGH Sir William Bruce had become the laird of a particularly fine property in 1675, when he bought the Loch Leven estate, and had become Sheriff of 'Kinrosher' and other things besides, he undoubtedly continued to consider his old house at Balcaskie his principal residence for at least another nine years. After all it was in 1674 that he employed George Dunsterfield to make three fretwork ceilings there, and letters show that right up to the day he sold the place he maintained house and land with meticulous care. In 1678, as we have seen, he was somewhat curtly dismissed by Lauderdale from his position as Surveyor General at Holyrood, but it was not until 1679 that he was formally relieved of all responsibility for the work on that project. We have also seen that Bruce's dismissal did not prevent the Magistrates and Corporation of Edinburgh from engaging his services on their public works, and in 1681 he seems to have been re-engaged in a rather unusual job, the restoration of Preston, or Priest Field House, between the City and the village of Duddingston.

This was the home of Sir James Dick, Bart, a wealthy merchant and a prominent Roman Catholic, so that when his grand home was burned down in an anti-papist student demonstration the Duke of York ordered it to be rebuilt at public expense, and apparently with Sir William Bruce as architect. Prestonfield House is now an hotel run by Sir James Dick's descendants, it is almost exactly as rebuilt except for a Georgian porch and a Georgian addition at the back. Its typical approach via a long avenue of trees remains, its intimate formal garden evocatively given over to peacocks; and its white harled walls are set off by dark stone quoins and architraves, the former copied from similar features at George Heriot's Hospital. One wonders, however, if Prestonfield's strikingly Dutch looking gables and perky, continental dormers were entirely new, or were perhaps merely replacements of what was there before?

If it comes to that, the quaintly serrated buckle-quoins from George Heriot's are really Jacobean in origin, so perhaps they too were a recreation rather than something quite new.[1] In any event, the interior of the house is entirely representative of the Restoration period in Scotland, in it to this day hang contemporary gilded leather hangings, and the heavily decorated rooms pervade an air of the slightly over blown, the 'too much' feeling that must have characterised court and aristocratic life at the time. The same plasterers as worked at Holyrood made the sumptuous ceilings at Prestonfield, and Jan Van Sant Voort carved the 'Grinling Gibbon' chimneypieces. Grinling Gibbon, of course, was only one of the many able Hollanders who made a good living in Britain then either as carvers, joiners or painters, and whose style was pretty much the same, even when it did not always come up to the very best of Mr Gibbon's work.

In the same year as Prestonfield was rebuilt Bruce's son John was given his 'Foy' (*feu de joie*), and sent abroad on 'The Little Tour in the company of his mother's kinsman, Dr. James Halket, to be 'finished.' The 'Foy' was usually given before marriage, and was the final stage in the thorough education of the sons of the Scottish gentry, when the young lairds-to-be travelled in France and the Low Countries, studied fencing at Angers, or Law at Bourges or Leyden, visited cousins at the Huguenot Academies at Saumur and Sedan, and sometimes crossed the Alps into Italy, though this was more an eighteenth century idea started by Sir John Clerk of Penicuik when he ran away from Leyden and created the fashion for 'The Grand Tour.' Mr John Bruce was away more than two years and dutifully and regularly supplied his father with detailed accounts of his expenditure and good works from such places as Antwerp, Brussels, Paris, Angers, Amsterdam and Nantes, (the two farthest extremities of his educational journey). It was from Paris, in November 1682, that he sent home to Kinross certain shrubs, flower roots, seeds, and 'Two gilt swords and two periwigs;' and when he returned in 1683 he had so thoroughly imbibed all that he had seen, and taken such good account of it, that for the rest of his life he was considered one of the finest gentlemen of his time and estate in Scotland.

The year 1683 was an eventful one in other respects, for it was then that the King's brother and representative in Scotland went south again. An earlier trip to London, made against the advice of Charles II, had seemed to show that opposition to his presence there had receded a little, and it might be safe to ignore the Test Act and return to Court. In practice this proved not to be the case, and the Duke, plus several Scottish attendants, beat a hurried retreat by sea back to Holyrood. Amongst those in the Lord High Commisisoner's party were Sir James Dick of Prestonfield, Bart, and Mr John Hope of Hopetoun, a cousin of Sir William Bruce's by marriage and father of the future first Earl of Hopetoun, who later employed Bruce at Hopetoun House. The ship, the 'Gloucester,' foundered on a sandbank off Yarmouth, and many lives were lost, including that of Mr Hope, whose son, then just two years of age, was subsequently erected to the peerage, in recognition of his father's courage in helping to save the life of the Duke of York. Sir James Dick's report states that the crew made straight for the only 'lifeboat' and would have left everyone else to their fate but for the lords in attendance who had to draw their swords in order to secure room for the High Commissioner (and his dogs); and in all 200 men were drowned.

The Duke of York's second attempt to end his technical exile in Scotland was assisted at the Whitehall end by the King's Mistress (the 'papist whore'), Louise de Querouaille, Louis XIV's spy at the English Court and the person chiefly responsible behind the scenes for furthering the Counter-Reformation cause in England. However, this 1683 return was nearly as disastrous as the previous one, and had it not been for the sudden death of 'Old Rowley' in 1685, brother James would have been sent packing up north again, indeed the plans for such an eventuality had already been made and approved, and it was then, no doubt, that the idea of his staying away more or less permanently was promoted. Leslie House, in Fife, (known rather pompously as Rothes Palace on account of its intended royal occupant) was prepared as a suitable retreat for the unwanted father of the Princesses Anne and Mary; but in the end he never came, the Long Gallery had been made longer than Holyrood's in vain, and many of Sir William Bruce's grander embellishments, if not wasted, were at least unnecessary.

Lady Bruce attended the Coronation of James II of Great Britain (VII of Scots) and Mary of Modena in 1685, and described for her husband the fireworks and other amusements, including the set-piece portraits in *feu d'artifice* of the King and Queen; which suggests that we have not progressed so very much further in that particular line since then. These were halcyon days for Bruce and his family, but they were to be of brief duration. In 1687 King James ordered the re-edification of the Abbey Kirk at Holyrood as a 'Catholick Chapell where divine service may be performed; and likewise be made capable of the ceremonies and solemnities of the most ancient and most noble Order of the Thistle'; but Bruce was not asked to assist and most of the work was 'prefabricated' in London and sent up ready by sea. It was very splendid, too splendid for the people of Edinburgh, who, a year afterwards, broke into the newly furnished Chapel Royal and destroyed everything they could lay their hands on; they even defiled the remains of Scotland's Kings and Queens, whose corpses were dragged from their resting places and displayed in the open.

In order to obtain possession of the Abbey Kirk for his own purposes, and for the use of the Knights of the Thistle, James VII had to find alternative quarters for the congregation then using the place. He did this by diverting a Mortification made at the time of Cromwell for the building of a chapel on the Calton Hill, and never carried out, to build the Kirk of the Canongate, an extremely handsome baroque fronted edifice designed by James Smith, son-in-law of Robert Mylne and subsequently, in the reign of Queen Anne, Supervisor of all the Royal Castles and Palaces in Scotland. Smith's works are often confused with Bruce's, and according to John Fleming, in his book of *Scottish Houses and Gardens open to the Public*, Colen Campbell is quoted as saying that Smith was 'the most experienced architect in that Kingdom [Scotland]'. This comes from *Vitruvius Britannicus*, where, however, a somewhat similar statement appears anent Sir William Bruce, who is mentioned as being 'justly esteemed the best architect of his time in that Kingdom [Scotland].' Smith certainly worked with and under Bruce. He probably built Dalkeith Palace for Anne, Duchess of Monmouth, and Hamilton Palace (now demolished) is accredited to him, as are Newhailes (his own house near Mussel-burgh), and Melville House, in Fife. Smith also had a hand in the enlargement of Drumlanrig Castle for the first Duke of Queensberry, another ploy with which Bruce has been associated, though again merely as adviser, not architect. It was finished in the last year of King James's reign, though begun earlier. I will have more to say about several of those quasi-Bruce structures in a later chapter and bring them in here chiefly to show how all pervading was the influence of the former King's Architect.

In any event, whatever else Smith did or did not do, with or without Bruce, the Canongate Kirk is entirely his, and deserves a short description here if only to demonstrate how variable is the fate of buildings and their builders; and to show as vividly as may be the kind of chaotic political and religious background against which architects and masons laboured in the latter part of the seventeenth century. James VII was, as is well known, a convert to Roman Catholicism, but as Duke of York and Charles II's Royal Commis-sioner at Holyrood he had gone out of his way not to offend his brother's extremely touchy protestant subjects. As King, however, 'another face of things was seen,' and James revealed his true colours, or, if that is too unfair, he foolishly acted on the advice of ill-informed Jesuit advisers. In Charles II's time the chief supporters of the monarchy had been the episcopalian gentry, and the presbyterians had had a pretty lean time of it. The new King, in order to strengthen the papist faction, deliberately encouraged the presbyterians to the disadvantage of the existing establishment, taking a calculated risk thereby, which, if successful, would in his opinion lead to the re-acceptance by the whole country of the Roman Obedience.

So rabid in his propagation of the Counter-Reformation cause did the King become that in less than three years he had alienated, or even dismissed, almost every non-papist supporter he had in Scotland (and England), and driven many of the others into retreat. His ostentatious setting-up of a popish chapel at Holyrood was typical of the tactless way in which 'James the last' provoked the opposition and embarrassed and exasperated his friends. As Duke of York he would never have done such a thing. His chapel was utterly wrecked by an infuriated populace before the mortar was properly dry, while the Kirk of the Canongate which he had provided for the dispossessed congregation of the old Abbey Kirk was untouched; it is very much alive today, having just been handsomely restored to something resembling its late seventeenth century condition. The King was surprisingly clever in his instructions to Smith in respect of this Church. He was to build it with a chancel and place for an altar, to be installed once the Romish faith had been reinstated as the official religion, meantime he was to block up the opening to the proposed chancel and await events. For nearly three hundred years James's chancel apse remained shut off from the main body of the kirk by a 'temporary' wall, and until after the Hitler War few people realised there was anything there at all. Then Mr Ian Lindsay, the architect for the restoration, took the bold step of having the wall demolished and putting in its appointed place not an altar, quite, but at least a doucely draped Holy Table. Thus were the intentions of a wilful King carried out. Not entirely as he envisaged, but carried out just the same!

Bruce and his newly married son John were at this time busily engaged on laying out the park and gardens at Kinross, and beginning on the House, which was to cost vast sums of money and to lead to straightened circumstances for the whole family, especially after the flight of King James and the mixture of suspicion and hostility Sir William Bruce had to put up with from the new government. From attending Coronations in London Lady Bruce was reduced to wearing out her old clothes at the elbows, and having to apologise for having 'nothing to wear' to her friends.[2] In 1688 Sir William was summoned to appear before the Privy Council and asked to account for his lack of enthusiasm for the regime. He refused to do so, and never again sat in the Scottish Parliament or took any part in official affairs after the dethronement of King James. He was one of the old gentry whose loyalty to the Stewarts could not be shaken, even if it meant dismissal losing wealth and position and possibly facing arrest. Bruce's main pre-occupation now was with architecture, and in 1691 he completed one of his most accomplished designs, the co-ordination and formalisation of his grandson's ancient castle at Craighall, in Fife. He achieved this by the usual methods of joining two antique portions together by a linking central screen, in this case an extremely proficient exercise in baroque patterns, with fine stonework and a carved pediment that would not disgrace an Italian palazzo. He repeated something in the same vein at the House of Nairne, in Perthshire, and on the garden front of Hopetoun House, plans for which he was asked to prepare in 1696 by Charles Hope of Hopetoun (Sir Thomas Hope of Craighall's cousin, and future first Earl).

Craighall Castle was blown up about ten years ago. It had stood empty for a long time and was thought to be dangerous, only an eagle finial survives, taken from his ancestral home to Hopetoun by the Marquis of Linlithgow and erected atop a pillar in the garden as a commemorative souvenir. In 1693 Sir William Bruce was imprisoned in Stirling Castle for still not appearing before the Privy Council and for his meaningful absence from Parliament. His wife, Mary Halket, voluntarily went with him. This year marked the virtual completion of Kinross House all but a few of the internal furnishings; but let me complete the rest of the story before turning to a full consideration of Bruce's masterpiece which must have a chapter to itself. He was released from prison quite quickly, being in a way lucky, since many of his acquaintances were taken to London and locked up in the Tower. In 1694 he was incarcerated again at Stirling, and in 1696 was re-arrested and confined in the strictest possible manner in Edinburgh Castle.

Bruce's first arrest, in 1693, had apparently been a mistake, or so the Mylne papers suggest, but mistake or no, he carried on his professional life as best he could. Three projects were in train (besides Kinross) some additions at Panmure, the completion of the steeple at Heriot's Hospital (for which he had prepared drawings nearly twenty years earlier but which, for some reason or other, had not been passed on to Robert Mylne to fulfil until now), and the improvement and enlargement of Craigiehall (not to be confused with Craighall), the Marquis of Annandale's seat in West Lothian.

James, fourth Earl of Panmure, had married in 1687, Margaret, daughter of the third Duke of Hamilton, and amongst Bruce's designs of 1693 was one for a marriage column of unique appearance. In fact, it has an oddly oriental look about it (perhaps not intended) being a free-standing, square pier, heavily rusticated in the French manner, about three times the height of the average gate pier, though not much fatter, and capped with a finely carved stone urn. On one side are the words, James, Earl of Panmure, 1694, and on the opposite, Margaret Countess of Panmure. The inscription is in bold capitals and was formerly gilded, but today this isolated remnant of other days and other ways, stands alone and uncared for in a field, its gilded glory gone. It is practically the sole survival from Bruce's time of the original Panmure House. The fourth Earl was nearly the last of his line; he was a staunch supporter of the House of Stewart, though dismissed from his post in the Privy Council by James VII on account of his lukewarm attitude towards the re-establishment of Roman Catholicism as the State Religion. He 'came out' in the '15 and entertained the Old Chevalier (James VIII) at Brechin Castle, his principal seat in Angus. On the failure of the Jacobite campaign he followed the Earl of Mar (his brother-in-law) and the *de jure* King back to the Continent and spent the rest of his life abroad. The Panmure Estate was sequestered and the house the Earl and his Countess lived in, which was partly built to Bruce's designs by John Mylne, is no more, only the gates (mentioned in correspondence of 1672 between George, third Earl of Panmure and Alexander Nisbet, mason) remain, otiose yet evocative in their baroque magnificence.

The Steeple of Heriot's Hospital does at last seem to have been erected in the summer of 1693, the draught having been considered and the order given 'to enter into Contract . . . for the finishing of the said steeple, and to make payment [to Robert Myll, Master Mason], of the soume of Three thousand and ane hundredth merkis Scots for doing thereof . . .' As for the Annandale project, it had a Hope association, for Henrietta Johnstone, the Marquis's only daughter, was to marry Charles Hope of Hopetoun and the Craigie-hall estate, which ran next to Hopetoun, eventually became Hope property. Lord Annandale, a prominent Scottish Judge (or Senator of the College of Justice) wanted Bruce to improve the internal working of his house by removing obtruding pillars in the hall and stairs and to install sash windows instead of casements. He wanted to be in the fashion in other words. His letter is a model of consideration and sense such as few architects then or now could normally expect, for it shows a remarkable understanding of the architect's proper place in relation to building, and rightly accepts his complete authority over the work. The Marquis of Annandale treats Bruce both as a reasoning human being and as a truly professional man. He does not order him about, nor attempt to intervene or counteract his instructions, even though he knew he had been in and out of prison and was not in the best of positions to attend to every small detail personally. 'I will give no directions nor order the alteration of annie thing in my building without acquanting you, hoping to have your approbation and consent.' What present day architect wouldn't give his eyes for such a client! 'I see you have made take away the pillar which was next the stair, which looks weill and makes more room to the stair . . . you know the less your look be bounded att your first entrie the greater is the satisfaction, besides it shall add extremelie to the light and pleasure of the staires. All this is very obvious to my sight . . . else I would not have ventured to have dealt so freelie with you in point off contrivance, and therfore I hope you'l give your directions and orders in this matter.'

The house which Bruce modernised for the first Marquis of Annandale was altered in the eighteenth century by William Adam and his sons, or rather the house itself wasn't much, the late Sir Robert Lorimer altered that. The Adam family went to work on the estate, building follies and grottos and so on, and thus the bulk of Craigiehall, unlike Hopetoun, which was hidden behind a large Adamesque facade, seems to have survived. Curiously enough, for more than two hundred years now, this delightful small mansion has been described as 'Adam,' even by its owners, and only within recent memory has anyone bothered to notice the monograms and date on the pediment which prove it was completed by 1699 (when William Adam was still a boy) and was the home of the first Marquis and Marchioness' of Annandale (a Fairholm of Craigiehall), not the second Marquis, who was Adam's patron and brother-in-law of the first Earl of Hopetoun. This second, bachelor Marquis was a typical product of what in England might be called the Burlington Age (in the north it was Sir John Clerk of Penicuik who set the fashion for things Italian and was labelled the Lord Burlington of Scotland). Lord Annandale was a great traveller, an aristocratic amateur artist, connoisseur and admirer of Italy, and it is largely due to him that Hopetoun House contains so many fine art treasures, he left them to his sister. He evidently found Craigiehall restricting and out-of-date, even with its 'six foott deep chasse windowes.' and brought in the Adam family to Georgianise parts of it, and decorate the park with temples and ruins.

There is a drawing of Craigiehall in William Adam's *Vitruvius Scoticus*, which may have contributed to the misunderstanding over authorship, though one would have thought the date, carved in stone, on both east and west pediments, sufficient proof against this. Craigiehall serves as the Officers' Mess of Scottish Command Headquarters. It is maintained extremely well and is still approached by the most magnificent 'yew avenue,' surely the best surviving in Scotland (actually yews interspersed with Cedars of Lebanon with a secondary row of oaks behind) The house is so patently Bruce, even at a glance, that the mistake seems almost inexplicable, unless deliberate, Adam being better known and more popular than Bruce.

There is some particularly delicate carving, inside and out. The entrance doorway, with its fruit and vegetable sculpture above, is delightful; while one of the principal chimneypieces, in what looks like the old dining room, is almost Grinling Gibbon, I say almost, because, although the wheatsheaves are there, (even the suggestion of peapods), the carving has not quite the feathery touch of the master: but it is good. A number of painted inset panels enliven the beautiful oak panelling, two of Edinburgh in the late seventeenth century, one of Windsor, and another, which is either of some scene in Annandale, or Craigiehall, before its rebuilding. The wrought-iron stair is superb, a twin, I should say, of one at Caroline Park, Granton home of Viscount Tarbet, legal confrère of the first Marquis of Annandale. There are two such staircases at Caroline Park, a very famous one, very rich and suspected of being of Continental workmanship. It is not that one which repeats itself at Craigiehall, but the one in the South Wing, built in 1696, which is native in every part, being made up of roses and thistles, and the odd tulip, the latter no doubt in tribute to William of Orange. The monogram of the first Marquis and his wife again appear as well. The craftsmanship here and throughout the house is outstanding, except that the original brass ball finials on the stairs have been replaced by crudely shaped, modern thistles. Bruce would have hated these, everything he did was so refined, it is his hallmark, and no detail was too unimportant for his attention.

In the grounds is some more fine carving, mostly late-Stewart, and a valuable sundial, contemporary with the Bruce house, cut by a man named England, of Charing Cross, Instrument Maker to Her Majesty (presumably Anne, but possibly Mary). Like the staircase it is one of a pair, the other being at Hopetoun where most of the carvers and others went on to. In fact, Craigiehall was being finished at about the very time work on Hopetoun began in earnest, and it really resembles a sliced off corner of the larger house. It is also one of the first mansions in Scotland to have a pedimented centrepiece, possibly not the very first, there was a rounded one at Craighall,[2] in Fife, circa 1691, and at Wemysshall, which Bruce designed sometime between being released from his second imprisonment in Stirling Castle, in 1694, and being locked-up again, in Edinburgh, in 1696. Wemysshall was a small country house, smaller than Craigiehall and about the same size as Auchendinny. It stood on the Hill of Tarvit, in the Parish of Ceres, across the Cupar Road from Scotstarvit tower, a particularly hale and hearty Fife laird's hideout, the eyrie in Jacobean days of Sir John Scot of Tarvit, famous cartographer and man of letters. His survey and notes on the Land and Islands of Scotland (prepared with the help of that gifted draughtsman and

Minister of Religion, Timothy Pont), were printed in Amsterdam in 1654 by John Blaeu. Scot's wife was the sister of the poet Drummond of Hawthornden, Scottish cavalier and the first Scotsman to write in pure English. Besides entertaining poets, wits and wags in his high tower overlooking the Howe of Fife, Sir John published a remarkable book, *Scot of Scotstarvit's Staggering State of Scots Statesmen.*

Wemysshall was formerly the property of the Wemyss's of Unthank and consisted simply of a well proportioned rectangle of masonry with a central pedimented entrance and stair window, one set of openings on either side and a hipped slate roof. The usual dignified effect that Bruce invariably achieved was produced here by his clever but sparing use of rustications and margins, plus the symmetrical disposition of handsomely coped chimneys. There was a pineapple on top of the pediment in place of the more familiar urn, bust or statue (or popular acorn, reminder of 'Oak-apple Day' and The Restoration). Pineapples became all the rage as a decorative feature after the first one grown in Britain was presented to Charles II (Danckert's picture of Mr Rose, the King's Aberdonian gardener, on bended knee before his sovereign, displaying the exotic growth, will no doubt be familiar to readers); and Bruce had several carved to go at Kinross and Hopetoun.[3] Wemysshall was pulled down in 1907 and rebuilt to the designs of the late Sir Robert Lorimer, who retained the spirit of Bruce, if not the actual substance, in his enlargement and rehabilitation. The house was then rechristened Hill of Tarvit and is now in the care of the National Trust for Scotland.

It was in 1696 that Bruce was approached to draw up plans for the park and mansion at Hopetoun, and construction work on the latter actually began in 1698, continuing until 1704. In 1698 also the old Duchess of Lauderdale, Bruce's cousin and the *châtelaine* of Ham, died. She had outlived the Duke by sixteen years and since his death had spent much of her time at Tunbridge Wells, 'taking the waters' for her gout. Indeed so frequently absent was she from Ham during her second widowhood that at the time of the 'Great and Glorious Revolution' William of Orange counselled James VII and II to go there until the troubles blew over. A suggestion which was turned down by the last Stewart King on the grounds that the house was then only partly furnished and was, in any case, 'a very ill winter house.'

When Sir William Bruce was 70 he re-married, taking as his wife Magdalen Scott, 'daughter of David Scott, brother to the Laird of Gallowsheills and relect of George Clerk, junior Merchant Burgess of Edinburgh.' This was the Jacobite lady who lived in the Citadel at Leith for nearly forty years, died at the age of 82, in 1752, and through whom, one imagines, Bruce obtained the commission to design a new house for Sir William Scott of Harden, on the banks of the Tweed. It is now the home of the Duke and Duchess of Sutherland and is known as Mertoun.

For continued non-attendance at the Scottish Parliament Bruce was formally expelled in 1702, ostensibly for maintaining that the Act to secure the Presbyterian form of Church Government contained things inconsistent with monarchy. In practice this was a sound observation (if he made it, which is doubtful), for how could a republican system which believed in parity of ministry, and did not recognise any authority other than God, accept the jurisdiction of worldly governments and rulers, or even the patronage of heritors, as church patrons in Scotland are called? The old man's place in Parliament was taken by his son, who, notwithstanding the fact that he had campaigned against the Covenanters under Argyle as a young man, was acceptable to the new government. Mr John Bruce voted for the Union with England in 1707 and was the first M.P. to sit at Westminster for Sir Alec Douglas Home's constituency. In 1708 Sir William Bruce was imprisoned yet again in Edinburgh Castle, but once more many of his friends fared worse, a hundred persons of distinction being sent south to the Tower; and at no time did the former King's Architect cease his architectural work or fail to keep up with his normal business affairs. He seems too to have been left in the Castle after others of his persuasion had been released. Indeed one gets the feeling that the powers that-were simply forgot to release him, and that for the last few months of his life he was as much away from his lodgings as in them.

Ostensibly Bruce was detained because of the rumoured arrival in Scotland of Colonel Hooke, the accredited agent at the French Court of James VIII and III ('King over the Water'), and the notion was held by a jittery government that the seventy-eight year old Baronet, well known but utterly harmless politically, might join with others in a plot to restore the House of Stewart. A private letter to Sir William Bruce dated June 10th 1708 confirms the situation, it is addressed to him at Edinburgh Castle.

'Sir — I was very much concerned before I received the favour of your letter of the 24th. April from the Castle of Edinburgh to find you were there with many of your countrymen; but knowing it could only be upon suspition, was in hopes when the French fleet was gon you would have been sett at liberty; and tho' as you mentioned you were sent for to London, I see in the publick newspaper call'd the *Post Boy*, you with soume others are respited, and I hope in order to prevent the trouble of an inconveinient journey depending on that, I venture to direct this to yourself . . .'

78

Wᵐ Bruce himself Archᵗ 1685   The House of Sᵗ John Bruce   G. Barlack delinᵗ   R. Cooper sculp

59   Kinross House as it appears in *Vitruvius Scoticus*

60   The plans of the house. Sir Wm. Bruce lived in
the Old Manor and gave the mansion to his son John

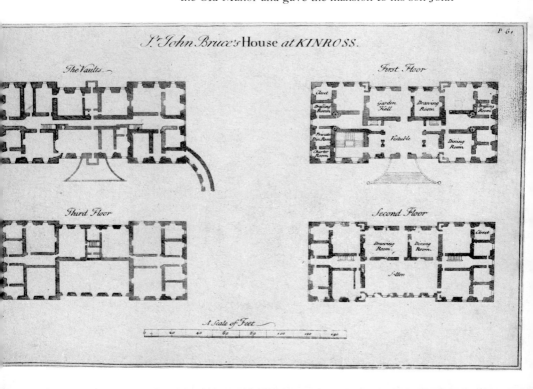

Sᵗ John Bruce's House at KINROSS.   P. 61

The Vaults

First Floor

Third Floor

Second Floor

A Scale of Feet

61 Wrought ironwork by Bruce's smith from Kinross and sundial by the Royal Smith from Holyrood at Drumlanrig Castle

62 Avenue leading from Drumlanrig's 'show-front with balusters and piers similar to those at Kinross

63 Looking down from a corner turret onto the entrance cupola at Drumlanrig. Note similarity to same feature at Holyrood but with ducal instead of royal crown

64 North front at Raith, near Kirkaldy. One of the first pedimented centrepieces in Scotland this house, completed about 1694 was afterwards much altered

65 View southwards over the Howe of Fife from Melville House, showing ogee roofed gazebos

66 Melville, the main façade, with side wings and pavilions

67 Detail pediment w
Arms of the first Marqui
Annandale, monogram
himself and his wife,
date 1699, at Craigiel
near Edinbu

68 Main entrance showing
refined and typical Bruce
mouldings and finishes

69   Midhope Castle, West
Lothian. Late 17th century
doorway

Formal entrance to
idhope, former seat of the
pes of Hopetoun

71   The garden front at Hopetoun House as designed
by Bruce (Circa 1700)

72   View westwards from the house towards Midhope, and Abercorn, with 'Queen Anne' sundial,
similar to one at Craigiehall, in foreground

73   Bruce's octagonal stair with characteristic carving. The actual
steps are of stone, with bowtel mouldings

74 Top landing at Hop
    toun showing more fir
    carvings and portraits
Mr John Hope and his wif
Dame Margaret, daught
of the Earl of Haddingto
parents of the first Earl
                  Hopetou

75 Back stairs with
contemporary wrought-
ironwork by Wm. Aitkin

Another epistle from the same person, a Mr Ruthven, to Sir William, thanks him for his great consideration even in prison, 'No misfortune to yourself or indeed trouble in my affairs ever makes you forget your great charity to me, as I find by your kind endeavours, even in your imprisonment.' The matter under discussion is the discharge of a small debt, and it is in this, the final letter we have from anyone to the aged and respected architect, that we sense, as perhaps nowhere else, his innate gentlemanliness, his quite unrepresentative character in a cruel and unkind age wherein cynicism was more a virtue than a vice and chicanery the rule rather than the exception.

1 The same curious pattern may be seen on the corners of Staneyhill Tower, former home of Sir Wm. Sharp of that Ilk, now a quasi-folly in the grounds of Hopetoun House.

2 'I have hardly any clos that I could be seen into ather lenen or wolene except on well knowne goune, bot for lenens none at all,' declared Dame Mary in 1696.

3 Both rounded and triangular pedimented features were introduced into his design for the garden front at Hopetoun, and survive.

4 The pediments at Craigiehall are also surmounted by pineapples.

Fontaine de Medicis, Paris

CHAPTER SEVEN

Kinross House

The most beautiful and regular piece of
Architecture in Scotland

IT WAS FROM a near bankrupt Earl of Morton that Bruce had obtained his Kinrosshire estate,[1] and it marched with the smaller property of Arnot, on the southern side of Loch Leven, which was already Bruce property. Arnot Tower survives, an ivy-clad ruin half-submerged in its creepers and closely surrounding trees, standing beside a modern house. The Bruce of Arnot Burial Aisle too, originally part of the auld kirk of Kinross but converted by Sir William Bruce to its present purpose when he built Kinross House, was restored in 1860 and an old stone with the date 1675, recalling the purchase of the estate incorperated. In an article published by the *Kinross-shire Advertiser* in 1932 it was stated that Bruce 'died at Kinross and was buried in the centre aisle of the old Parish Church, now part of the Mausoleum built by Thomas Bruce of Arnot in 1859.' It is curious, however, that no memorial to their illustrious ancestor was erected by the Bruce's of Arnot at the time, and that no reference to Bruce's interment appears in Mr Marshall's notes.

With the Loch Leven estate went the Lordship of Regality and Justiciary of Kinross, the hereditary Sheriffdom of the shire of Kinross and the office of Keeper of Loch Leven Castle. It was an Earl of Morton, it may be remembered, who was responsible for the safety of Mary, Queen of Scots when that unfortunate lady was imprisoned in the Castle in 1588, but whose guardianship did not prevent the Queen's escape at dead of night. From the beginning of the fourteenth century until the middle of the sixteenth this castle in the middle of the loch was the home of the Douglases of Morton, but by Queen Mary's day there also existed what Sir Robert Sibbald in his *History of the Sheriffdom of Fife and Kinross* (circa 1710), described as 'a Neat Manour,' a typical turreted, crow-step-gabled Scotch Baronial laird's tower. This was called the 'New House of Lochleven,' and was itself to be supplanted by a newer house when

Sir William Bruce built his classical mansion slightly to the south west of it. Sibbald, incidentally, was a medical practitioner with appointment to King Charles II. He was born in Fife and renowned as a natural historian and geographer as well as a physician; his accounts of the contemporary (mostly Queen Anne) scene in his native Scotland include interesting comments on several of Bruce's houses, notably Balcaskie, Kinross and Hopetoun. The 'New House of Lochleven' he mentions became Bruce's home while Kinross House was being built, and he returned to it in 1700, when he presented the larger mansion to his son and heir, John Bruce, and his son's wife, Christian Leslie, daughter of the Duke of Rothes, widow of the third Marquis of Montrose and mother of the first Duke of Montrose.

Actual work on the new Bruce mansion at Kinross did not commence until about ten years after the purchase of the estate, indeed, repairs to the 'New House' are recorded as having been made to 'the plaster on the stair that enters Sir William's study' as late as 1687; and long before the mansion was completed (about 1693) the gardens had been planted and had become famous. Sir Charles Lyttelton, writing to Sir William Bruce from London in the last year of the reign of James VII and II, says he hears 'Lady Lauderdale's gardens at Ham are but a wilderness to be compared to yours at Kinross.' If this is true then Bruce's gardens really were splendid, for John Evelyn, himself a celebrated and erudite horticulturist, familiar with the greater gardens and houses of France and Italy, described the House and garden of the Duke of Lauderdale at Ham as 'inferior to few of the best villas in Italy itself . . . the Parterres, Flower Gardens, Orangeries, Groves, Avenues, Courts, Statues, Perspectives, Fountains, Aviaries, & all this at the banks of the Sweetest River in the World, must needs be admired.' The 'Sweetest River in the World' is still there, and both house and gardens at Ham have been preserved in a reasonable state since the date of Evelyn's entry in his diary in 1678. Whether the garden at Kinross, and the house for that matter, surpass them is an arguable point. I know both, and find them quite different, which makes comparison difficult; but so far as perfection of layout and formal vistas are concerned Kinross has it every time, and I rather think the house too, if viewed in a purely classical, Palladian context.

Almost complete records exist and are in part available to the public in the Register House in Edinburgh of the history and building of what Daniel Defoe called the 'most beautiful and regular piece of Architecture in Scotland,' and which Sibbald declared was 'unsurpassed by few in this country.' Down to the last nail we know the details of the creation of Kinross House, who created it and at what

81

cost; but first, perhaps, it may be as well to say something about the house today, describe its unique situation beside Loch Leven for the benefit of those who may be unfamiliar with the place. The house itself lies at the exact centre of an axial line of half a mile in length, with Loch Leven Castle at one end and the Town of Kinross at the other. On the loch side, to the east of the space occupied by the famous gardens, the area is precisely equivalent to that of the open court on the town, or west side, and the castle closes the view perfectly from the central windows of the house. On a clear sunny day, when the Lomond Hills rise up pleasantly in the background, and the water around the island on which Loch Leven Castle stands is blue and inviting, the illusion of being in northern Italy, possibly at the southern end of Lago Maggiore, is very strong. One must not exaggerate the similarities, but they are certainly there, and probably were intended to be, for it was not by accident that Bruce sited his 'noble palace' where he did 'on the banks of this lake and adjoining the town of Kinross.'

Stendhal once wrote of Lago Maggiore, 'Quand par hasard, on a un coeur et une chemise il faut vendre sa chemise pour voir le lac Majeur.' On the right day one could say the same about Loch Leven seen from the gardens at Kinross House. Unhappily the climate is not Italian, and very often on the rare days when the gardens are open to the public, it rains unmercifully (I recall at least two such occasions); but as always there are compensations, and the ancient castle of the Douglases of Morton merits a little romantic mist occasionally to put it back in its true Caledonian and non-Mediterranean context! Bruce's attraction to the historic as well as the scenic value of the site is shown by his setting of an old heraldic stone, presumably from the Castle, in the wall of one of his new garden gazebos. The waters of Loch Leven, incidentally, are extremely shallow, which makes them eminently attractive to anglers, a point emphasised by Bruce in his 'Fish Gate,' at the bottom of the garden facing the loch. The design of this is a typical example of the architect's employment of novel features, of his 'being before his time,' at least so far as Britain is concerned. His icicles and "freezings" here predate any others in the north, and clearly derive from De Brosse's Medicis Fountain in the Luxembourg Gardens in Paris.

Above the opening to the 'Fish Gate,' between a pair of quite extraordinary cornucopias (more like sausages than horns and probably meant to suggest eel nets or something like that), is an upstanding basket of fish, containing, it is said, the seven varieties normally to be caught hereabouts. They have been listed by the late Walter Montgomery as, salmon, gelletroch, (char), speckled trout, grey trout, ledue (blackhead), perch and pike. The eel fisheries were discontinued early this century as the result of a dispute with the Loch Leven Trustees, but the salmon fishing is renowned and fills local hotels with devotees in the season. It is interesting to note too that the Reddendo, or symbolic return offered to the Sovereign by the lairds of Kinross for holding their lands from the Crown, was a basket of fish.[2] The two lions, supporting the shield of Bruce and Halket respectively, and formerly atop the main gateposts to Kinross House from the town, sit on either side of the gate, about a third of the way along the garden wall.

The House, a quarter of a mile from Loch Leven castle, is built upon a slight rise, the formal garden falling gently down to the 'Fish Gate' and forming a square enclosed on three sides by high park walls, broken twice to provide vistas. The best of these 'peeps' opens to the north, where a sizeable gap between ornamental pillars topped with urns reveals forest trees in a sort of Watteauesque setting, ideal for a *fete champêtre*. There is nothing quite the same anywhere else in Scotland. Near 'the gap' used to be a vinery, and beyond that lay the 'New House of Lochleven,' (Sibbald's 'Neat Manour' and the predecessor of Kinross House). The garden walls are supposed to have been built, in part, from rubble from the old 'New House,' though this seems unlikely if Bruce went back to live there in 1700 and it was not demolished until about 1723. The vista on the south side is less expansive, giving onto the old Kirk wynd, the Kirk of which has long since been demolished, being represented solely by the Bruce of Arnot Aisle and kirkyard, set on a spur running out into Loch Leven south west of Kinross House. The west gateposts bear polygonal sundials cut by James Hamilton in 1686, and in each side enclosure are charming little gazebos with ogee roofs. The one on the east has the heraldic stone from Loch Leven Castle let into the masonry above its keystone arch, and both have the monograms W.B. M.B. (William Bruce and Mary Bruce — or Magdalene Bruce, one may represent his second wife), carved within handsome swags.

The flowered finial to each of the garden gazebos is finished in wrought iron, beautifully worked. There is not much wrought iron at Kinross, not belonging to the seventeenth century at any rate. The balcony on the south front is characteristic and genuine, resembling one at Caroline Park and others at Drumlanrig, but the entrance gates, alas, which must have been the finest part of all, are no more. This period saw the apotheosis of Scottish wrought iron work based on the mortice and tenon principle of construction, of which two outstanding examples remain at Traquair House, in Peeblesshire, and the gates (formerly at Gogar House, Midlothian) at Sauchieburn House, Stirling. These were inspired by Continental models and would not have disgraced a chateau entrance in the France of Louis XIV. Their wonderfully curvacious but essentially natural detail is wholly satisfying, and an ingenious expression of the correct use of the material involved, which makes the loss of the Bruce gates at Kinross particularly regrettable, They must have been the very best of their kind. Nothing, absolutely nothing has survived, not a drawing or a plan, a sketch or anything, so that there was nothing, not even a suitable description to guide those who had to provide new gates this century.

Kinross House is a large building, though compact. It has four stories, plus a mezzanine floor cunningly lit by small windows on the north and south elevations and reached by 'page's stairs.' The bottom floor consists of 'vaults' and the top of attics, the lower being lit by square windows set in rusticated stone work *a la française,* the upper by neat little windows between the eaves and the classical cornice. The house is entered via a *perron* of easy steps that curve out, like the side wings, to greet the visitor. The present porch was added by Sir Basil Montgomery by simply projecting Bruce's design outwards a few feet from the facade and making his pilasters pillars. Above is the sumptuous and extremely tricky piece of carving undertaken by the two Dutch sculptors Boyse and Van Nerven, cut into the face of the masonry after it had been erected; while over the central window is a cartouche with the Arms of Sir William Bruce and Mary Halket. On the south front over the central balcony there is some more fine carving in relief in the same French-baroque manner, and another cartouche, this time with the Arms of Sir John Bruce and his spouse, Christian Leslie. The main elevations are simplicity themselves, four rows of five windows balanced by four rows of three windows, the latter in pavilions slightly forward from the centre. The chimneys are part of the overall design and comply with Bruce's known capacity for placing them so as to make the house warm, and look well; they are very elegant and help to raise the height of the building, an effect enhanced still further by a central cupola.

There are several innovations at Kinross, the mezzanine floor and 'page's stairs,' the introduction of corridors (nearly all previous houses had relied almost exclusively on through circulation from room to room); and the imaginative use of curved wings, concave nearest the house and convex beyond the two ogee-roofed garden-houses. There is much fine panelling and carving inside, painted overmantels and at least one delightful corner chimneypiece (some have been replaced). The saloon, on the first floor over the front door, is a double cube and must have been the picture gallery once (records speak of portraits of Charles I and Henrietta Maria by Van Dyck and other seventeenth century masterpieces since removed). The open

84

court on the main, west facade, is the same size as the garden on the
the east, and is a complete square composed of gravel and grass,
with an opening for the avenue, a quarter of a mile long, leading to
the new gate at the town end of the park. To the north side of the
square court, behind the avenue, is the stable block in the design of
which Bruce reverted to indigenous forms, using swept dormer
windows and harling. The 'doocot' is a splendid exercise in circular,
conically capped Scotch architecture, refined yet rural and of a naturally
lesser magnificence than anything closer to the house. The ogee
pavilions at either end of the stable block are noble yet thoroughly
domestic, the fine grey iron-streaked stonework being allowed to
create its own patina of ageing beauty. Correspondence shows this
block was roofed as early as 1686, when the house had only reached
basement level; and there was probably a balancing counterpart on
the southern side of the main avenue, if existing remnants of
masonry are anything to go by.

In the 1761 edition of *A Tour thro the Whole Island of Great
Britain* a reference to Kinross House contains this sentence, 'The
Town . . . lies at a lettle distance from the House, so as not to
obtrude upon its Privacy and yet so as to be ready to wait upon its
call.' It is a happy phrase for a happy and judicious juxtaposition of
laird and populace, mansion and burgh, which, unfortunately, has
recently been discarded in an ill-conceived, if well meaning, attempt
at modernisation at the gates. A scheme in which the douce stone
houses with their good grey slates on one side of the entrance lane
have been replaced by bright, red-roofed bungalows which can be
seen glaring down the quarter mile avenue right to the door of the
Bruce Mansion. The gaudy out of place colours and gimmicky use of
varied but irrelevant and unfunctional facing materials are unlikely
to tone down for many a year to come, if ever. So far the opposite
side of the entrance space has been left more or less as nature and a
more proprietous generation intended, let us hope the mistake now
made on one side will quickly be seen for the horrid blunder it is and
not increased in magnitude by any foolish and unthinking repetition.

The author of the second edition (1738) of the 'Tour' waxes
lyrical in praise of Kinross House, quoting Dryden:
> 'Strong Dorick Columns form the Basse,
> Corinthian fills the upper space;
> To all below is strength, and all above is grace.'

which, *pace* Mr Marshall, is not strictly accurate, for there is no
Doric at all in the architecture of Kinross, only huge Corinthian
pilasters at the corners and a touch of Ionic on the porches east and
west. Perhaps one can excuse the allusion, however, since the writer
may have been thinking of 'the Great Doric Gate,' described as 'a

large Gate of curious Architecture' by Sir Robert Sibbald in his *Sheriffdoms of Fife and Kinross* in 1710. Tobias Bauchop, Bruce's mason, built the gates in 1684 (that is several years before any walls of the house appeared) according to the drawings and a timber model supplied to him by Sir William. 'Draught' and model, as well as gates and gateposts have all gone, the 'living' gates being destroyed by Thomas Graham of Kinross, a latter day laird, in a fit of religious mania, under the influence of a local preacher, and builder, who convinced him of the 'evils of decorative art.' He would have succeeded in having other fine things removed or mutilated as well but for the intervention of the townsfolk (who took away the mason's scaffolding) and the Almighty (who called the laird to higher things). This was in 1801, Since when Kinross House has remained intact all but its 'Dorick Gates;' and when Sir Basil Montgomery restored house and grounds, early this century he had perforce to imagine what the gates might have been like, and he went, or so it would seem, to Melville House, repeating on either side of his new entrance the ogee-roofed pavilions that perform that function there.

In the first edition to the 'Tour,' dated 1722, Defoe accurately describes Kinross House as being 'built of Free stone; adorned with columns of the Corinthian Order; the office under ground vaulted, and the galleries of communication paved with stone are the noblest I have seen anywhere.' He goes on, 'the great staircase is the same as at Melvil (this is not absolutely true, though there is a "facial resemblance"); the great salon that goes from it is two storey high with a lanthorn at the top as at Montagu House at London' (the first Duke of Montagu returned from a visit to Versailles in 1680 determined to emulate 'Le Roi Soleil' as far as he could). Defoe mentions the Stewart portraits in the salon, then continues; 'The great avenue from the town of Kinross is the noblest you can imagine. You enter it by a pair of stately stone gates, in a quarter of a mile you reach the outer court, with pavilion, stables and coach house in each corner' (these are now confined to the north side, but in view of Bruce's addiction to symmetry it is only to be supposed that there were once buildings on both sides, as the author of *Robinson Crusoe* says). 'There are two other avenues from the outer court, that run to the lake on one side, and through a wood on the other; there are also some curious vistas cut through this wood (a reference to 'the gap' almost certainly). This lake is full of fish, particularly the finest fish in the world (salmon?).

The 1761 edition speaks of the house being 'all beauty; the stone is white and fine, the Order regular the contrivane elegant, the workmanship exquisite.' Nine years later the antiquary and naturalist Thomas Pennant visited Kinross and made the following comment;

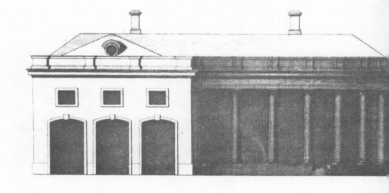

Ca: Campbell Delin:

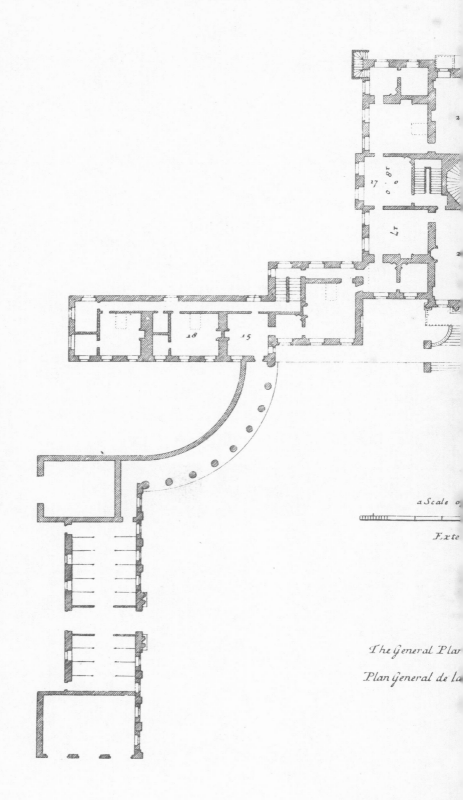

18

15

17

17.0.0

a Scale o

Exte

The General Plan

Plan General de la

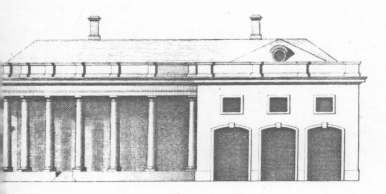

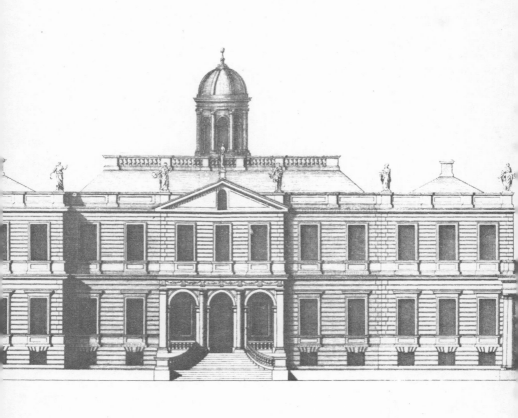

8o Feet ⊢ㅣㅣㅣㅣㅣㅣㅣ   Extends 316

aſt Front of Hoptone houſe in the Shire of Linlithgow in Scotland the Seat of the Rt Honble the Earl of Hoptone
. to whom this Plate is moſt humbly Inſcrib'd . Invented by Sr Wm Bruce .1700

Elevation Orientale de la Maiſon D'Hoptone dans la Comté de Linlithgow en Eçoſſe .

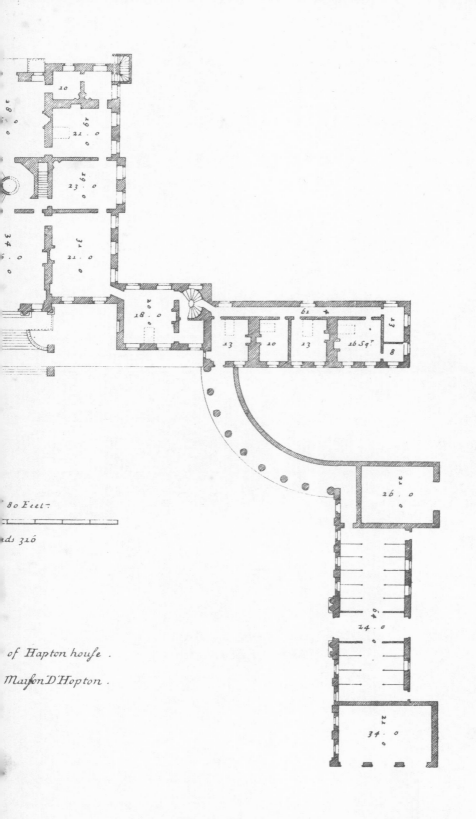

10

21 . 0

23 . 0

21 . 0

18 . 0

13   10   13   16 Sqᵗ   8

61   4   7

80 Feet

ds 316

26 . 0

24 . 0

of Hapton houſe .

Maiſon D'Hopton .

21 . 0   34 . 0

'Not far from the town is the House of Kinross built by the famous architect Sir William Bruce for his own residence, and was the first good house of regular architecture in North Britain;' while Sibbald's most direct reference to the House of Kinross mentions 'a stately building which for situation, Contrivance, Prospects, Avenues, Courts, Gardens, Gravel-walks, and Terraces, and all Horticulane Ornaments, Parks and Planting, is surpassed by few in this country.' The plans and drawings in *Vitruvius Scoticus* are only slightly different from what was actually built, and William Adam seems to have taken them from original sketch plans. In fact, it is remarkable that any architect of standing should have been so consistent in his intentions as Bruce was when building his own house, for without clients to keep him in order, to tie him down, he might have been tempted, as so many other architects have been when working for themselves, to take too many rabbits out of the hat, follow too many odd brainwaves, so that the final result would have come out either unfinished or extravagantly overblown. Sir William Bruce of Kinross succumbed to none of these temptations and he must, surely, be counted amongst the most brilliant, if not *the* most brilliant example of his *genre* in this particular respect in British Architectural history. For what other architect has succeeded in building a virtually perfect house, as planned in his mind over a number of years, without seriously amending it, either at the last minute, or as the work progressed? With only very minor changes Kinross House today is as he designed it.

As we have seen Sir William Bruce, Bart, (then of Balcaskie) purchased the Loch Leven Estate on which he was to build his new house, his masterpiece as it turned out, as early as 1675, whilst still in the midst of rebuilding the Palace of Holyroodhouse for the King. He planned the gardens and park first, as accounts for levelling in the garden commencing in the year 1680 prove. The final reckoning came about 1693; and one reason why the work took so long to complete was that payment to tradesmen had to be made largely from rents which the architect had difficulty in collecting. This resulted in his having to drag things out on occasion, and straighten his living, though somehow or other he managed to get his monetary affairs in order over the years, so that by 1690 he could say; 'I have pay'd all my annual rents diminished my debt and advanced my building not far from finishing.' We know, however, it was not only Sir William who had to go canny as a result of the great burdens imposed in building Kinross House and laying out its splendid gardens (the ones that made Lady Lauderdale's 'but a wilderness') for his wife, albeit willingly, shared his restraint too, as did his son John when the time came. The gardens alone are said to have cost Sir

William and his heir more than £400 a year to keep, after they were laid out! I have not had the temerity to ask the present proprietors how much it costs them or indeed how they manage to keep Kinross up as they so successfully do — a motor mower is a boon, but it obviously cannot do everything!

The ashlar, or squared facing stone, which Defoe described as 'white and fine . . . the workmanship exquisite,' is actually a delicate shade of grey, patinated here and there with iron streaks, and it came from the Cleish Hills, to the south west of Kinross. It is particularly strong and fine and can scarcely look a lot different today from when it was first used here in the last decades of the seventeenth century. The facades at Kinross are quite clean and smooth, almost new looking, even now. Only where softer red sandstone from Bruce's own quarry at Clayhill was employed in the building (in the garden wall and gazebos and other ancilliary structures) is there any appreciable sign of wear. The Clayhill Quarry no longer functions, and in the restoration of 1902 and afterwards, another source had to be found; but the general effect is still homogeneous and authentic looking. The earlier documents unearthed and codified by the indefatigable Mr Marshall give a list of costs for labour and materials, and compensation paid for damage done by carting the stones from the quarries to the site (the carters seem to have knocked down people's gateposts and stone dykes!). The common wage of the quarrymen is given as 5d. to 6d. per day; and ashlar supplied for the 'great gate,' Dials, Lions heads, Globes, Acorns, was priced at 1d. per foot. Of course these figures are virtually meaningless unless translated into modern currency, which is well nigh impossible, except by the most complicated and not wholly reliable methods. Comparisons between trades may be a better guide, for labourers, like quarriers, received an average of 6d. per day while leaders of carts only 4d. or less.

The amount of compensation for damage caused by carts bringing the stone to Kinross was decided by a neutral committee and paid out regularly without demur. A number of cases are mentioned in the papers, including one dated 1688 for 'nyne years damnadges by cairts betwixt Nivieston (the Cleish quarry), and Kinross . . . £10 Scots the first five years, the last four years 20 merks, . . . besides some firlots of feid corn at a mark the firlot of oats the encrease being past by.' Considerable damage was also done to crops by the carts, all of which Sir William Bruce had to make good, He had to repair the gates at the quarries as well (one would have thought this an unnecessary burden); and a 1687 item from the old Charter Room at Kinross discharges Bruce from providing 'ane bole of oatmel for ane year's winning of stones in his quarel (quarry).'

The chief mason at Kinross was Tobias Bauchop, from Alloa, whom Sir William Bruce employed a great deal. Bauchop, as we have seen, made the 'great Gates' according to the architect's drawings and model. He was paid approximately 18 pence (English money), or 16s. 8d. Scots, per day, which was about the price paid to ordinary masons in Edinburgh. Here at Kinross assistant masons had to be content with 10d. per day. As the work proceeded wages went up, as they always seem to, and the Bauchop family, Tobias and his brother John, were advanced to 1s. 8d. daily, their assistants, including a son, to 1s. 3d. Over the years 1684–1686 the Bauchops did work costing Bruce nearly £2500 Scots, and this, plus £75 in 1683 and £224 on scaffolding for the 'great Gate,' makes quite a tidy sum for those days, namely around £2800 Scots, or £235 sterling. The gazebos were built by a local mason, James Anderson of Kinross, 'summer seats' they were called.[3] They cost £100 Scots each. Anderson also assisted John Hamilton, an apprentice mason to James Smith (architect son-in-law of Robert Mylne), to erect the polygonal sundials. He hewed bases for the dials, for pineapples, flamepots and urns at 3s. 4d. each (sterling).

Other masons taken on under the Bauchops of Alloa include Mungo Wallace, who is interesting not only because he built the two gates, one on either side of the outer, or paved and grassed court at Kinross, but because he probably carved the handsome Steedman gravestone in old Kinross Kirkyard, on the edge of the park. Wallace was the step-son of John Steedman, yet another local mason, and the tombstone, dated 1703, bears the family Arms. James Mercer, mason, came to work at Kinross from St. Andrews in 1688, with an apprentice, they being paid £40 Scots per month for two years employment. Mercer was responsible, amongst other things, for the bold and beautiful balustrading along the top of the concave wing wall linking the two side pavilions, or ogee-roofed gazebos, at the main entrance to the house. Marshall goes on to say that Mr Mercer was made an honorary burgess of the City of Perth in 1692, where he died in 1713. In 1881 he had a descendant living, Mrs Haldane-Duncan-Mercer-Henderson, of Fordell Castle, in Fife. The Hendersons have since gone elsewhere, but Fordell, a particularly interesting place, is still inhabited. It has a famous garden and Renaissance Chapel.

The part played in the completion of the mason work at Kinross by the Dutch carvers Peter Paul Boyse and Cornelius Van Nerven has already been dealt with. An English stone cutter is also mentioned in the documents pertaining to the building of Kinross house, his name is not given and there are no other particulars except that for 38 days of 'dyet,' he received 8d. per day. A visit to the old kirkyard will also reveal the tombstone of Robert Watson, Cooper (who died in 1715), noticeable by having a cooper's implements, heading knife, compass and adze carved upon it. He made 'meikle tubs' at 2s. apiece, buckets at about 7d. A day's work girding the buckets earned him 10d., and the iron girds cost 1 English, or 12 Scots, pennies each. Of the wrights, or joiners, John Fair, (also a mason), was overseer at 1s. per day. He first arrived at Kinross in 1685 and was fed in the house, and outside, when he was allowed 5d for meals. John Honeyman, wright, sawed 'wanscott and flooring, cut broom among the fir trees in the moors,' and did other odd jobs, for 8d. per day, while Alexander Eizat, the Edinburgh wright with experience at Holyrood, measured up the sizes for timber to be bought in Holland through the Kirkcaldy wood merchant Provost Williamson, for wainscoting, doors, windows and other finishings in the house. He made the timber roof, cupola and the 'chassie' or casement windows, charging £748. 2. 0. Scots for his labours. The actual note of his account has survived for 'wright work at Sir William Bruce's house of Kinross beginning Jan. 1690 thenc to the first of Dec. for the said year.'

Transport across land presented considerable problems before the advent of rail, I say rail purposely for during the last ten years, during which rail has tended to be superceded by road, we ourselves have been rapidly getting back to the same expensive and cumbersome ways as our seventeenth century forebears. It was easy enough to bring the goods by sea from Rotterdam, or even from Leith to Kirkcaldy or any other Fife port, but the difficulty was to get them overland. The Kinross papers speak of 71 horses being required to bring about four hundred floor boards from the coast, each horse averaging six boards per journey. The distance of between twenty and thirty miles there and back took two days and a night, and although some of the smaller timbers could be carried in carts larger items had to be dragged by the horses all the way. Really big 'trees,' however, were reduced in size at the port; Bruce having to pay for this himself. He began buying timber from Provost Williamson as early as 1683, and by 1688 had added Mr Watt, 'marchant at Dundee,' to those who supplied him with planks and 'trees' (mostly oak). One gets the impression that Scots hardwood was mainly used, but Continental softwood, Memel pine especially, was still coming in fair quantities from Holland to Kirkcaldy right up to 1693, when Customs dues were paid by Bruce on 'twell Ells, nine ells, deals, wanscott planks and knaples'.

In the same year, the one in which Sir William Bruce was first taken into protective custody in Stirling Castle, Mr William Erskine, Governor of Blackness Castle and Lt. Col. John Erskine, Governor of Stirling Castle (both sons of the Earl of Mar) sent 'deals for the use of Sir William's buildings at Kinross at £54 Scots the hundred.' Here the timber was conveyed by water, down or across the Forth as the case might be, to Limekilns, a small port near Culross on the Kincardine (Bruce) estates, thence by land. John Erskine, incidentally, later became fifth Earl of Mar, the notorious Earl whose allegiance to the Royal House of Stewart wavered under James VII and II, and who served for a time as Secretary of State to Queen Anne; though he returned to the Jacobite fold to lead the Fifteen Rebellion, and to spend many years of exile in France, Holland and Italy. He married the daughter of the Earl of Panmure and, as we have seen, filled in his idle hours abroad improving and recording in detail James, Duke of York's plans for a new, classical town of Edinburgh. He also be-friended James Gibbs, the Aberdonian architect, and paid for his journey to Rome, where the future designer of St. Martin-in-the Fields attended the lectures of Carlo Fontana at the Earl of Mar's expense. Whether Bruce arranged these supplies whilst 'inside' the Castle at Stirling is not known, but Lt. Col. Erskine's Governorship would seem to prove pretty conclusively that Lauderdale's crafty attempt, made on behalf of Charles II, to dislodge the Mar family from their hereditary keepership, failed.

The successor to the Duke of Rothes as Chancellor of Scotland was James, fourth Earl of Perth, a convert to Roman Catholicism and one of King James's foremost adherents. 'His faith hath saved him,' was how one cynical contemporary described the Earl's sudden conversion. Be this as it may, it led to his having to flee with the King, in 1688, when, however, he was created 'titular' Duke of Perth. He was the inventor of the thumb-screw; but more importantly in the present context he gave Sir William Bruce a licence in 1684 'to win skellie,' or slates, for roofing Kinross House. The licence does not seem to have sufficed, for a year later a contract was made with slaters in Doune to provide materials and labour from time to time, when required. These Perthshire slates were specified as 'the best black skalzie of Monteith,' and it is perhaps worth commenting here that slates in Scotland were then rather a refinement. They were not used generally for small houses, or in the country. We have seen how the Duke of Lauderdale insisted on more than one occasion that he 'positively will have blue skailzies.' Hatton House, on the other hand, his brother Charles Maitland's grand residence, was pantiled, and this was by far the most common form of roof covering, especially in south and east Scotland. [4] In Edinburgh nearly all the buildings except Holyrood, the Castle and churches, were red-pantiled which must have made it a much brighter place than it is now, while in the country districts, other than by the east coast (where imported Dutch tiles were used) the ordinary houses were thatched with reed, or sometimes merely covered with divots (turf). In Angus and other suitable districts stone slabs took the place of slates or pantiles for the better buildings, and these were often sent south by sea, to Fife and beyond. Before Kinross house was properly roofed temporary 'defets,' or turfs, protected the place from the weather, and in 1686 one James Meldrum supplied '700 divits to thacke the Icce house and the lettel foulls houses that stands in the orchard.' Marshall says the ice house used to stand 'at the South East corner of the Garden to the north of the Church Yard.' Imported pantiles, by the way, originally arriving as ballast in colliers plying between Culross and the Low Countries, were augmented in the 18th century by tile factories owned and set up by William Adam, the Kirkcaldy 'architect.'

The principal plumber at Kinross was Alexander Eizat, who did the lead work on the gazebos. Two more Edinburgh plumbers came to put lead roofs on the east porch and the west balcony, and to lay the roof of 'the Principall house at Kinross 1923 stones of lead, in the year 1690,' for which £25 sterling was paid, plus 4s. 10d. for drink money. The copper globe on the top of the cupola was supplied by James Miller, coppersmith of the Canongate in Edinburgh, at a cost of £17 Scots, on 6th of Sept. 1690. It weighed 11 lbs. 'Incident and Contingent Charges de bursed by Mr Kennuvie' (James Kennoway, Sheriff-Depute of Kinross and senior Chamberlain to Sir William Bruce) include one 'To James Burn for goeing twyse to Edinburgh for the great Copper Globe and bringing it and other things over £3. 7. 0. Scots (5s. 7d.)'

Plastering appears to have been a thirsty business for almost the first item on the plasterer's schedule is a penny a day for drink money (the price of half a pint of the best ale). Wages were 1s. 2d. This was for local workmen, George Dunsterfield, the King's plasterer, whom Bruce specially brought over to make the elaborate fretwork ceiling above the main staircase, received more, though not so much more as one might expect, only three times the lower standard, that is, 3s. 6d. daily. Lime for the plaster was obtained nearby in the Lomond Hills, just across Loch Leven, while good hair with which to bind it came from Leslie, to the east, being purchased by Bruce from Henry Kid, Shoemaker, at 6d. a stone, as well as from Robert Mill, parchment maker of Milnathort (the next small town to Kinross). The ovens used during the building were in part kept going by birch logs from the Kincardine estates, but fires to burn the lime were made of small coals from the Fife coalfields, Keltie and Rescobie being mentioned in the accounts. The coal was sold at from 1½d. to 2d. a load, peats by comparison (used to dry the timber), cost 3½d. to 4d. 'Great Coal' sold at 3¼d. per load.

James Horn, (Horn is still a well known Fife name)[5] the smith responsible for the 'Swipe,' or 'Great Gate,' the 'South Yeat,' or 'Little Gate' (that is the water gate), and the balconies, of which only one on the east exists, facing the garden (the west balcony was probably never made), charged £178. 14s. Scots for his work and two hundred and sixteen stones of Iron. The latter was bought in various places, locally, and at Leith, and as far away as Perth. Horn must have been both proficient and able, judging by the ironwork remaining at Kinross, the garden balcony and balustrading to the steps below, finials and few other items that have survived. It was either he or someone close to him who later went to work at Drumlanrig with Paul Boyse and Van Nerven and several more from Kinross. He did none of the fine ironwork at Hopetoun, however, and is unlikely to have made the very elaborate and sophisticated iron stair panels of the north wing at Caroline park; it was not his style, which was essentially old Scottish.

The 'Iron Gait' for the 'Chirter House dor' and the lock for it was made by the Royal Smith, John Callendar, and amongst other itinerant craftsmen employed by Bruce was James Alexander of Leith, who painted the seven panels of the fine timber staircase at Kinross.[6] This mobility of labour is perhaps understandable in the higher grades of work people, who followed the most eminent architect of the day on his different ploys, going from there to assist his successors and pupils. It is rather less understandable to find a similar constancy of employment in the more permanently based workers and suppliers of materials, Isabelle Fermer, for instance, 'nail wyfe at Pathhead, who provided Sir William Bruce with nails over a number of years, at both Balcaskie and Kinross.

The most favoured wall covering of the period, judging by what remains in many rooms at Ham and some of the contemporary rooms in Prestonfield House in Edinburgh, was leather hangings, gilded and painted. They represented the wall-paper of the day, and were considerably cheaper than old fashioned tapestries, as Alexander Brand, 'Marchand at Edinburgh,' is at pains to explain in a letter of 1692 to 'The Mutch Honoured Sir William Bruce.' In this he refers to 91¼ Skins of 'Gold Leather Black and Gold' which he supplied for the 'Love (low), Dyning roume,' and 68½ skins of 'Gold Leather pearle gronde' for the Drawing roume (at 48s Scots the skin).

'Youlle ffynde,' he says, 'your two shutte of Gold Leather Hangings does not amount to above 26 Sterling and 5s, and one shutte of the coursest arrase would have cost more and wold not have done so well or Leasted so Longe bot I assure you I take it asse a great honor and favore that you are pleased to have any esteem of my worke and make use of it in severall Roumes of your house (which is admired by everiebodie).'

Brand also supplied Bruce with bed furniture and pictures, which suggests he must have run a shop of sorts, perhaps an early form of 'Liberty's,' only on a small scale. He retained the architect's confidence and custom until the year 1700. He must also have proved his point about the cheapness and serviceability of gilded leather hangings, for after providing those for the low dining room and the drawing room at Kinross he subsequently received 20s. Scots per skin for 33 skins of 'blew comon gilded laether,' (besides the cost of 'squating walting making up and nailes') for the 'Little Tobacco roume.' One likes to think of this as the small room with the corner chimneypiece on the right just off the main entrance, but the plans neither confirm nor deny the possibility. In fact, the drawings in *Vitruvius Scoticus* show seven modest sized rooms with corner fireplaces on each of the two main floors, and since then many of these smaller rooms have been run together for convenience sake. The drawing room mentioned by Alexander Brand, however, is still in existence (though not used as such) and is marked on the plan as next to the 'high dining room,' that is on the *piano nobile*, backing onto the Salon; The laich, or low dining room was probably the tiny one next to what is now a cloakroom at the foot of the stairs, but which used to be the Charter Room (the old drawings labelled it 'Private Dining Room'). A third dining room, also on the ground floor but larger, is shown near the little room with the one remaining chimneypiece, lending some credence possibly to the idea that here was 'Bruce's 'Little Tobacco roume.'

Bruce and his son John planted an enormous number of trees, as many as 100,000 by the year 1700, on the Kinross estate, including 300 chestnuts which came from France in John Bruce's luggage (he wouldn't have been allowed to bring them in nowadays!). James Shanks, who helped in the planting, was employed as principal gardener and forester by Sir William for thirty two years, receiving an annual salary of £62 Scots (about 5 gns. sterling) plus six bolls and two firlots of meal. He had under him three or four assistants who besides wages and oatmeal were paid shoe bounty at 2s. 5d. per pair. A number of bairns were also employed as weeders at 3d. a day. One of James Shanks' and Mistress Grizel's bairns, Mary, who died at the age of five, in 1685, is commemorated by a typical, ornate late Stewart tombstone near the entrance to the old Kirk yard at Kinross. It is said to have been carved by one of the masons engaged on building the house, and bears this inscription;

"The way shoe's gone we cannot shun,
    Ending hir days ere weill begun.'

Only Sir William Bruce has no memorial in the same ancient graveyard, in the same company as his faithful servants and members of his family.

76 Charles Hope, first
Earl of Hopetoun, at the
age of 13. Portrait by
Medina in the Collection of
the Earl of Haddington

The Bruce dining room
Hopetoun. Formerly the
oon, or garden room

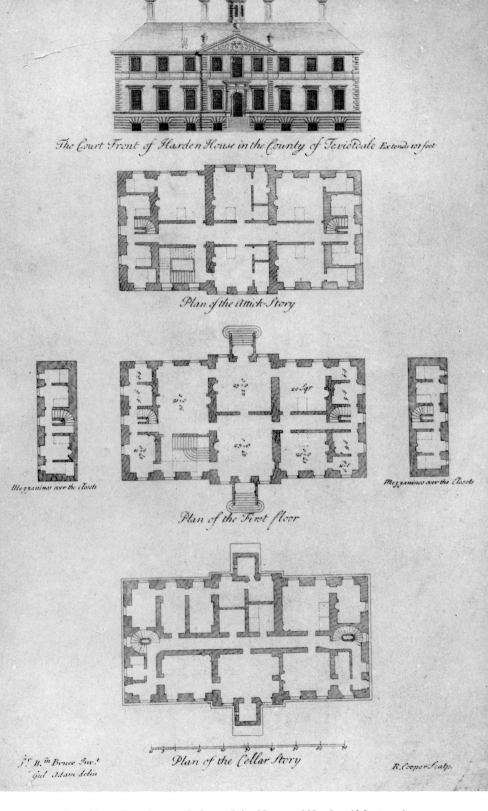

The Court Front of Harden House in the County of Teviotdale Extends 101 feet

Plan of the Attick Story

Mezzanines over the Closets

Plan of the First floor

Mezzanines over the Closets

Plan of the Cellar Story

Jr. Wm Bruce Invt
Gul. Adam delin

R. Cooper Sculp.

78   East elevations and plans of the House of Harden (Mertoun) as
they appear in *Vitruvius Scoticus*

79 Mertoun from the south west showing wing walls
and main front as recently restored

80 Detail entrance. Note Scott of Harden crest in
pediment

81　The tower of the Old Tolbooth, Stirling, designed by Bruce in 1702

82　The Stirling Tolbooth in its setting, with buttress of the Kirk of the Holy Rude, left foreground

83   The House of Nairne, Perthshire. 'Built by Wm.
Lord Nairne and destroyed by his nephew James,
Duke of Atholl.' Lord Nairne's drawing at Blair

84   Auchendinny from the north

85   Auchendinny was Bruce's last and smallest house.
View showing main front and part side pavilion

86   Detail entrance with remnant of low wing wall

87 'Hope's House,' or the Hopetoun Aisle, Abercorn Kirk. Before restoration

88 The same in the course of restoration. The Earls of Hopetoun were buried below, their descendants gather for church above

89   The Hopetoun Aisle in its setting at the east end
of Abercorn Kirk

90   Inside the kirk. The Hopetoun gallery, or 'loft'
showing squint through to retiring room and the
laird's achievement

The Bruce Aisle, all that now remains of the pre-Reformation kirk of Kinross, has no mark of any kind to suggest his ever having been laid to rest in the vicinity; though there are many stones and epitaphs to his contemporaries, descendants, and masons, and others connected with running his estate and building his house.

¹ Litigation continued in the Court of Session for over 21 years, and was one of the reasons for Bruce's straightened circumstances later on, and consequent inability to complete the whole of the interior of Kinross House.

² An old brass box presented to Sir Wm. Bruce by Charles II, and once containing the Charter of Kinross, was left by Mrs Philpott (formerly a Miss Bruce and the last descendant of the Bruces of Kinross) to the Rev. James Stewart of Stukeley, whence it came to the Chief of Clan Stewart, the present Earl of Galloway.

³ One of these, on the south side of the garden, was destroyed in a recent gale, when scores of fine trees were also lost.

⁴ Many of the houses at Kinross are still pantiled, though slate predominates, and thatch has disappeared altogether. Thatch may yet be seen, however, in neighbouring districts in Fife, notably at Auchtermuchty, near Falkland.

⁵ The fine wrought iron rail to the service stair at Raith House, near Kirkcaldy, Horn's home town, is typical of his work.

⁶ This refers to imitative 'grisaille' work on the wall side of the stairs, not the balusters themselves.

Craighall, Fife (now demolished)

CHAPTER EIGHT

Hopetoun and the last decade

THE LAST FEW YEARS of Sir William Bruce's long and busy life were, architecturally speaking, the busiest of all. Coming out of prison at Edinburgh Castle in 1696 he immediately began work on plans commissioned by the young laird of Hopetoun for a fine new house beside the Firth of Forth and a magnificent park to be laid out around it. Sibbald's account of 1710, written six years after the completion of the work, speaks of the future first Earl of Hopetoun (ennobled in 1703, he was only 15 years of age in 1696 and the contractual documents were signed on his behalf by his mother, and tutors) as acting on the advice of his cousin, 'the Lord Rankilor (Sir Archibald Rankeillor, a Law Lord and brother of Sir Thomas Hope of Craighall, in Fife), Sir William Bruce, and Mr Alexander Edward, Great Masters in Architecture and Contrivance of Avenues, Gardens and Orchards.'

Though plans were drawn up in 1696 actual building does not seem to have commenced until two years later (very probably the park was begun first) and Colen Campbell, in his *Vitruvius Britannicus*, gives the dates of erection as between 1698 and 1704. The house was built to the designs of Sir William Bruce, 'justly esteemed the best architect of his time in that Kingdom (Scotland)', says Campbell, and goes on to praise Hopetoun's various parts. 'There is a noble salon over the Hall — well finished and sumptuously furnished.' He refers to the very good stone with which the building is faced, its rustications, 'in the French manner' (a favourite with Bruce). He also mentions a big stone cupola over the octagonal stairs. The stairs remain, but the cupola, now only glazed, is almost entirely masked by William Adam's false balustrading and heightened roof line, done after 1721 on the advice of the second Marquis of Annandale, the Countess of Hopetoun's much travelled, *dilettante* brother. Campbell gives the ground plan and main elevation of Hopetoun as Bruce designed them, and one cannot help wishing it had been left alone and not enlarged by an inferior 'architect' (Adam was really only a glorified mason with none of Bruce's good taste, or sense, and no great knowledge of how to use the classical orders, which he tended to pile up at random). William Adam's architecture was less Palladian than Bruce's, more but poorly Vanburghesque. He utterly lacked that restraint which was so apparent in Sir William Bruce's best works, he was no patrician connoisseur but a builder with a little knowledge, and on the make. He had been Bruce's apprentice, possibly, and at least some of the craftsmen employed by him had either survived from the Bruce era or had been trained, like him, in the Bruce tradition, so that even when he went wildly astray in his design, the workmanship in stone and timber and iron usually remained first rate. It is this, on the whole, that saves the William Adam front at Hopetoun, gives it a grandiose *cachet* not wholly lacking in nobility; though it does not make it an improve-ment on what went before. The garden front is still mainly as Bruce designed it, that is a gentleman's house for Mr Charles Hope, not a palace in the Roman style for the first Earl of Hopetoun. It could never have been what this enormous house has since been nicknamed, the 'Versailles of Scotland.'

Campbell's drawing shows a particularly handsome building, quite grand enough one would have thought for any Scottish Earl, newly belted or no. 'A stately House with Avenues on all quarters,' as Sir Robert Sibbald declares in his *Linlithgowshire*, 'The principal Avenue openeth from the East, with Large Office houses and regular planting upon each side; this, when the Gates are all open, gives a Prospect through the Inclosures near a Mile Long. The House stands in the Center; the Courts are large, and there are fine Gardens and Orchards about the House, embellished with Waterworks and Jettoes.' The Bruce layout largely remains, and notably the Avenues spoken about. As usual he sited the building on some outstanding natural object, in this case Inchkeith, many miles away in the middle of the Firth of Forth; so that if one looks straight out from the entrance steps, down Sibbald's 'near a Mile long Prospect,' the view passes down the middle of the Firth of Forth, under the Forth Railway Bridge (the new Road bridge is off-centre and rather spoils things now) to Inchkeith and the open North Sea beyond.

On the garden side five vistas exist, two on the same line as the garden front of the house itself, that is, to the immediate south and north; the first is onto Staneyhill with its 17th century tower, since made into a Folly, but which was once the ancestral home of the Sharps, or Shairps of that Ilk, including Sir William Sharp, King's Cash Keeper to Charles II. The second vista lies straight across the Firth of Forth towards Dunfermline. Two other radiating views lead

97

respectively to Blackness Castle, and to the deer park; while a wide expanse of grass in front of the house leads past a handsome *rond point* through the trees to reveal the hill upon which the house known as the Binns is built (in Bruce's day it was the home of Tam Dalyell, cavalier founder of the Scots Greys).

Inside Hopetoun there is still a considerable amount of Bruce work, and the bills show that both Tobias Bauchop of Alloa and Alexander Eizat were employed. The finest of the State Rooms, panelled and beautifully proportioned, are by Bruce, as also is the octagonal staircase, a *chef d'oeuvre* so far as interior design is concerned. The stone steps are of the bowtell type, that is with the nosings returned down the sides (a typical Scotch feature which Bruce used even on the ceremonial staircase at Holyrood). The balustrading is of wood, with some very fine panelling on the walls, decorated with carvings in what is loosely called the 'Grinling Gibbon' manner. Of course, Gibbon, the genius whom John Evelyn discovered existing in poverty and obscurity in Deptford and brought to King Charles II, did not invent a style. He was probably of Dutch extraction, as were nearly all the best carvers of the day, and it was the Continental baroque style in which they excelled, and which is here seen in a particularly impressive and successful form. There is a corner chimney piece in the State Dressing room, but none of these rooms possess elaborate fretwork ceilings such as Bruce installed in earlier houses, instead the enrichments are confined almost entirely to ornate woodwork surrounds, swags, columns and architraves, and the ceilings are mostly simple coombs. Good proportion is the keynote in all the Bruce part of Hopetoun rather than undue reliance on elaborate decoration.

Apart from adding a completely new and largely false upper storey of pots and statuary to the east facade of Hopetoun, refacing the 'show' front and building entrance steps which rise alarmingly, without any rail, straight from the immense gravel and grass forecourt to the front door, William Adam altered the curve of the colonnaded wings Bruce had built on either side from convex to concave. For most of the eighteenth century he and his sons were kept busy making other improvements inside and out, gradually transforming the late Stewart mansion into a thoroughly Georgian one, all except the garden facade, which hidden from view behind its tall screen of masonry to the east, remained more or less intact. There are, however, still a number of Bruce touches in and around the house, the State Rooms, as we have noted, are still mainly his, not the Hall but certainly the octagonal staircase and carved panelling; and behind the scenes are the service stairs, masterpieces of seventeenth century design with the most marvellously expressive wrought-ironwork. The blacksmith here was William Aitkin, a local master at his craft and presumably one of the last, as well as the best. In the grounds will be found the twin to the fine sundial at Craigiehall (on the Annandale estate) plus a number of amusing gazebos and garden features which assuredly belong to the first stage of Hopetoun's creation. Cheek by jowl with the present estate office, for instance, is an old out-building with rusticated quoins and windows, margins, moulded cornice and gentle bell-cast roof, all in the inimitable Bruce of Kinross manner, the manner; which he employed in 1708, when, after finishing the house proper, in 1704, he was called back to build the Hopetoun Burial Vault and Aisle, and make the Laird's loft in Abercorn Kirk.

Abercorn village and Kirk stand beyond the great central avenue looking west from the garden side of Hopetoun House, on the same line as Midhope Castle, which is about a quarter of a mile further on and was in 1710 described by Sibbald as 'a fine Tower-house . . . one of the seats of the Earl of Hopetoun.' The 'baronial' castle enjoyed a face-lift about the same time as Bruce was employed on the new big-house and used to possess a contemporary oak staircase and much fine panelling, It is approached via a typically Brucian arched gateway and was, until comparatively recently, occupied by tenants on the Hopetoun Estate. Unhappily, since being taken over by the Civil Defence Corps it has been rendered uninhabitable and positively dangerous, and must now, I fear, be written off altogether.

Before Hopetoun House was finished Sir William Bruce had already undertaken three new designs, his smallest but most exquisite little house at Auchendinny, near Penicuik, in Midlothian; Harden, or Mertoun, on the banks of the Tweed near St. Boswells; and the Tolbooth and Steeple at Stirling. The Records of the Royal Burgh and former Capital of Scotland, at Stirling, state that in pursuance of a motion by the Council to rebuild the Town House and Steeple one Harry Livingston, a mason, was sent in March 1702 to consult with Sir William Bruce, taking 'ane exact account of the breadth and length of the ground along with him,' and instructions to bring back Bruce's 'draught or sceme of the work.' Building commenced in 1703 and a year later Livingston, assisted by John Christie, wright, had completed it. Parts of an older Tolbooth were incorporated in the new one, but the overall effect is uniquely classical, with Bruce's usual lugged architraves, fine Renaissance entrance and steps to first floor, ashlar masonry, rustications and unexampled patrician dignity. Inside a certain amount of late Stewart panelling and contemporary chimneypieces remain, even an inset landscape painted by one of the many itinerant Dutchmen with whom Sir William Bruce was associated. The tower is especially evocative and now, apart from the Mid Steeple at Dumfries (copied in 1705 from Stirling by our old friend Tobias Bauchop of Alloa) has no equal in its period. Its plain but graceful stone base is topped by an engaging timber and lead cupola with distinctly Netherlandish connotations, not entirely dissimilar from that crowning the entrance tower at nearby Cowane's Hospital, built in the reign of Charles I, and very like pictures show the top of the tower of the Tron Kirk in Edinburgh to have been before fire destroyed it.

The street outside used to be nicely cobbled and led up to the Castle in much the same way as the Lawnmarket in Edinburgh leads up to Edinburgh Castle, but Broad Street, as it is called, is now tar-macadamed and nasty, though the old houses roundabout have been expensively restored and new ones are in keeping. In front of Bruce's Tolbooth is a fine Mercat Cross surmounted by its original Unicorn. The Stirling Tolbooth, which no longer serves its old purpose, is in part occupied by the *Scottish Tartan Information Centre*. The Centre has a large and extensive library and many records and documents concerning tartans and Highland dress; it carries on a considerable correspondence with Scots folk everywhere. I suppose this is a good use for the handsome eighteenth century Tolbooth, it is better than no use at all and better, no doubt, than continuing as a prison and antiquated Court Room.

William Adam's *Vitruvius Scoticus* gives the plans and court (garden), elevation of Harden House as designed by Sir William Bruce, and begun in 1703. It shows a compact country mansion with a central pediment, fine steps, and cupola; a minor Kinross, possibly more like Moncreiffe, and with the inevitable lugged architraves, rusticated facings and margins, well disposed chimneys (none at the gable ends) and hipped roof. At the centre of the pediment is a shield surrounded with scrolls and foliage bearing the Arms of Scott of Harden, 'or, two mullets in chief, and a crescent in base, az,' while on the other facade, not shown by Adam but recently restored, the Scott of Harden Crest, 'a mermaid proper, holding in her sinister hand a mirror,' is carved over the entrance doorway within a smaller porch-pediment. Three pineapples now crown the corners and centre of the main pediment in place of the ornamental urns shown in the drawings, but perhaps these were only made to look pretty. in *Vitruvius*. In Georgian times unwieldy additions were made to Harden, so unwieldy they actually overshadowed the Bruce house; and they were not even symmetrical. One part was erected to help contain pictures from the fabulous Bridgewater Collection, which included several valuable Italian masterpieces, notably Titian's *Diana and Acteon* and *Callisto exposed*. These two pictures were painted in 1559 and were destined for Philip II of Spain. They were

100

to have been part of the dowry of the Infanta whose hand Charles I failed to win; but they went to France in 1704, when Philip V gave them to the Marquis de Grammont. Thence they passed to the Regent d'Orleans, whose descendant sold them, as a pair, to the Duke of Bridgewater in 1792.

When the fourth Earl of Ellesmere restored Mertoun, as the House of Harden had come to be called by 1913, the original foundation stone of 1703 was unearthed, on it was engraved: 'FOUNDED THE 10 DAY OF JUNE 1703 YEARS BY SIR WILLIAM SCOTT OF HARDEN AND DAM JEAN NISBET HIS LADY.' Sir William was Member of Parliament for Selkirk and presumably a kinsman of Magdalen Scott of Galashiels whom Sir William Bruce married as his second wife in 1700. His house has recently been refounded by the removal altogether of the unwieldy Georgian and neo-Georgian wings, so that externally, at least, if one turns a blind eye at the positioning of some of the chimney stalks and one or two other not easily altered features, Mertoun is as near Bruce's design as it could ever have been during the last two hundred years. It is unfortunate that the interior could not be salvaged, but except by gutting it and starting all over again, which no owner could be expected to do, this was not possible.

Today we have the two main elevations to enjoy once more, in soft dove-grey-to-pink stone of the most endearing and homelike quality, the front sitting down nobly, sideways onto the river Tweed at a particularly beautiful bend, and facing, with its low, wing walls and garden houses fully restored again, a long view towards the border hills behind Melrose. In the grounds, surrounded by trees, is Mertoun old Church, also a marvellous old Doocot, dating from before the Union of the Crowns, and the original Mertoun House, which is mostly a seventeenth century structure with steep roof, crowsteps and dormers. Many of the fine pictures from the Bridgewater Collection, displaced by the reduction in size of the house when restored to its original proportions, are on semi-permanent loan in the Scottish National Gallery in Edinburgh. Thus King Charles I's coveted Titians, which he lost through playing about with the Duke of Buckingham in Madrid instead of getting on with his wooing, are in Scotland after all, and unparted, as always.

The small mansion of Auchendinny, which Henry Mackenzie, known variously as 'The Scottish Addison' and 'The Man of Feeling,' Scott's particular friend, rented between 1795 and 1807, stands back from the Edinburgh to Peebles road, (via Leadburn,) at the end of a formal clearing in the trees, just past Milton Bridge. The estate was bought in 1702 by a Lanarkshire lawyer, John Inglis of Langbyres, Writer to the Signet, and the house, designed by Sir

William Bruce, is still occupied by his descendants. In fact, it was to an Inglis, Henry Mackenzie apprenticed himself at the beginning of his legal career, and to another he was tenant at Auchendinny. The smallest and last of Bruce's houses it remains more or less as he designed it. It seems to have taken quite a long time to build, although modest, 5 years in fact; but the result is a splendid little place, containing in miniature the whole essence of Bruce's style and taste, his reticence, his sense of dignity and fitness for purpose and his practicality. Looking down the grassy opening between the trees from the main road it sits there perfectly in position; all is grace, tranquility, repose and good taste. Again as so often, we have here the work of a gentleman; a gentleman in his seventies but still very much alive and on top of his profession. [1]

Auchendinny House, which is built of a most interesting purply-red stone, may have been meant to be harled, for around the windows and at the corners are the appropriate offsets and margins to take it, though it does not look as if it was ever done. The front door has a typical pedimented surround and is entered at the top of a small curving stair. On either side are low curved wing walls linking the house with the two handsome side pavilions; and these have delicately moulded architraves, lugs and cill brackets, the gentlest expression of baroque you ever saw. The chimneys are centrally placed above the supporting walls to the inside stairs, and thus, as usual, help to keep the house warm whilst adding to its external decency. In his *Anecdotes and Egotisms* Henry Mackenzie mentions Bruce's chimneys specifically. 'Bruce of Kinross,' he says, 'was remarkable for his construction of private houses, that they never smoked. I have lived thirteen years in one of his buildings at Auchendinny, seven miles from Edinburgh, the only chimney of which that smoked was that of the kitchen in which some modern alterations had been made.'

There may have been an earlier house, or small castle on or near the site of the present house, the 'Toure and Manor place' mentioned in records of 1557; and this would seem to be confirmed by the existence of older masonry and low vaulted cellars below Bruce's building, plus a turnpike, or spiral stair, possibly re-used by the architect, at the back of one of the side pavilions. The plan is simplicity itself, a front door, entrance lobby, and plain stone stairs, mounting between solid stone walls in scale-and-platt fashion, that is up to a half-way landing then round and up again. The ends of the beautifully tooled and exposed stonework being rounded to suggest a column. On either side is a room. The upstairs plan is virtually the same as the ground floor except for a tiny panelled closet at the front, over the lobby, and a dressing room off the principal bedroom. There are several fine contemporary moulded stone chimneypieces in the house, quite a deal of good panelling, some in oak the rest in Memel pine, and in the principal bedroom and dressing room painted insets similar to the ones at Brunstane. I do not think it possible that these could actually have been done by the same Dutch artists whom the Duke of Lauderdale sent up to Scotland in 1673, after all we are now in 1703 to '07, though they may have been painted by someone employed more or less contemporaneously at the Bruce-inspired house of Caroline Park. Amongst the subjects depicted at Auchendinny, Roslin Chapel and Castle are easily recognisable, others are more tantalisingly suggestive than obvious, Arthur's Seat, a Border Abbey (Melrose?), a baronial castle beside either the sea or a loch (Tantallon?). The panelling here too is painted in the correct blue-green shade of the period (as recently restored by H.M. The Queen's personal choice in the Long Gallery at Holyrood); not scraped bare and allowed to get the worm and rot away as so often happens.

At Auchendinny, as at Brunstane, some original glazing has survived between thick astragals of the 'Queen Anne' era (it is, of course, a rare example in Scotland of a genuine Queen Anne House). Also in keeping with the precepts of the age and Sir William Bruce's especially, the house is sited with a vista opening onto a notable natural curiosity, so that looking north from the front steps, almost in the centre of vision, the rounded summit of Castle Law rears up before one. There is an Iron Age fort on top, earthhouse and ditches, and one of the best vantage points in the Pentland, or Pictland, Hills. In the course of time a slight bend has developed in vista, but there can be no doubt what was intended and what is very nearly still there today.

The owner of Auchendinny is not only very lucky in having such a lovely view and such a splendid Bruce house in which to live, but such a small and manageable one, the only one of its size and date, and in a perfectly delightful setting. The main facade faces north, a point which classical designers considered best, and which is surely better than turning everything towards the south, and the sun, whereby curtains and carpets are ruined, and the glare in one's eyes prevents one from enjoying the landscape. The classical idea was to look out from northern facing windows, with an even light in the rooms, towards a scene upon which the sun played. This is how things are at Auchendinny. A Queen Anne House by Sir William Bruce sited, before its time (as the Georgians would have sited it) with the main elevation to the north.

In the Tulliebardine Room at Blair Castle is a drawing of the House of Nairne, which was begun in 1706, when Auchendinny was yet unfinished. The drawing was made by James Nairne, grandson of the second Baron Nairne of Strathord, and on the back is an inscription that reads: 'The House of Nairne — of Strathord — built by William Lord Nairne and destroyed by his nephew James Duke of Atholl.' It shows a large four-storeyed house of characteristic Bruce design, rusticated, boldly symmetrical, well proportioned, a central pedimented feature, cupola, hipped roof, sidewings and vast, enclosed forecourt. It was begun after a fire in the previous mansion, and finished, windows and chimneypieces included, but not all the internal finishings, in 1710, the year of Sir William Bruce's demise. From the drawing it looks as if it must have been pretty big, perhaps Bruce's largest country house. Indeed it was called 'the glory of Strathord,' and its destruction is a great loss, to say the least. The Nairnes were devoted adherents to the Royal Stewart cause, the first Baron Nairne suffered imprisonment in the Tower of London throughout the period of the Cromwellian dictatorship, and his son-in-law, the second Baron Nairne (a Murray by birth but by arrangement the bearer of his wife's rights as heir to her father) was likewise imprisoned in the same gruesome place in 1708 (following the scare of the same year when 'The Pretender' was supposed to have arrived by sea in the Firth of Forth).

The second Lord Nairne, actually the fourth son of the first Marquis of Atholl and Lady Amelia Stanley (and, it is worth recalling, the grandson of the indomitable Countess Charlotte of Derby, heroine of the Siege of Latham House and of Sir Walter Scott's novel *Peveril of the Peak*) did not, so far as is known, actively support 'Bonnie Dundee,' but he did refuse to take the oath of allegiance to the Government of William of Orange, and like Bruce he never sat in his seat in Parliament after the fall of the House of Stewart. He may have been directed in his choice of architect for the new house on the banks of the Ordie burn, near Perth, by his wife, Margaret Nairne, one of those remarkable Scottish ladies who combined in their natures all the more usual feminine accomplishments with a decidedly masculine sense of purpose and intense loyalty to the native line of Kings. She is said to have been a pupil of Bruce's, to have studied architecture with him at Kinross; if so she can certainly be claimed as the first Scottish woman architect, perhaps the first woman architect anywhere! The *Chronicles of the Atholl and Tulliebardine Families* mention her architectural activities and in particular how she designed some new parts of Blair Castle and was responsible for various structural improvements to the existing building. She made drawings for the new Court of Regality Court-House at Logierait, near Pitlochry, shortly after her kinsman by marriage, the second Marquis of Atholl, had been created a Duke, in 1703. It was reckoned a very fine building at the time, one of the best in Perthshire; but unhappily it did not survive the eighteenth century any more than the new House of Nairne did, which Bruce designed at her husband's behest, with her money, in Strathord.

I have visited the site of the House of Nairne but could find absolutely nothing to show exactly where it once stood, the Ordie burn is there, of course, and a small bridge over it, a country cottage beside, and what may, I suppose but one cannot be sure, be the remains of the old mill mentioned in contemporary descriptions. There are no signs of there ever having been any sizaeble avenues of trees (which there certainly were) and not even a large enough piece of flattish land, a platform if you like, upon which to lay out so expansive a house and forecourt as drawn by Lord Nairne's grandson. Yet particulars of the House of Nairne, its building and attributes are fully recorded by James Nairne himself, 'The Glory of Strathord' was built near the former seat of the Nairne family and cost in the region of £5000 (sterling).[2] Sixty masons were employed on the work (this must mean assistants and apprentices as well) and every Saturday night they went to the Inn at Loak nearby (I could not find this either, though the village survives) where, at Lord Nairne's expense, they received one large oat cake, a salt herring and a pint of beer each.

James Nairne's description, complementary to his sketch, says 'There were thirteen large rooms on a floor (four floors) besides closets with vents (this sounds as much like Lady Nairne's idea as Bruce's, for she was always a practical woman). It stood in the middle of a very improveable estate, six miles in extent, larger than the Island of Guernsey. The plantation of trees, natural wood etc., sold at a moderate price, would have been double the purchase money which was paid for it when it was ultimately brought to sale.' Lord Nairne 'came out' in the '15, was captured and sentenced to death and his property sequestered by the Hanoverian Government, and although his son was able to get it back, when he too 'came out,' in the '45, the Nairnes were finally dispossessed. There was a sale, however, later on, when relatives and friends deliberately made low bids in order to help the family to regain their former property, but the second Duke of Atholl, taking selfish advantage of the situation, bought the lot at a bargain rate, and demolished the house. He then sold everything he could for the best price he could get. No wonder his nephew had some hard things to say about him. One or two features from Bruce's House of Nairne were incorporated in the King James Sixth Hospital at Perth, including the cupola or clock tower, which the Duke of Atholl graciously presented to that institution and which it still graces. We are told the house had 365 windows, which may or may not be precisely true, that the ground floor was all vaulted, that there were 'cellars, kitchens, pantrys, bakehouse, brewhouse, dairy and other conveniences, with a large brook or stream of water near it sufficient to turn a mill, which was conveyed to the house in many shapes.' The stream is there alright and probably a bit of the mill, but that is all, no sizeable trees, nothing but arable land and much open space.[3]

Though both Lord Nairne and his son took part in the Rising of 1715 and Lord Nairne was condemned to death, the latter sentence was subsequently suspended and means were found, while the title was attainted and neither father nor son permitted to reside on their estate, to provide for the needs of Lady Nairne and the daughter of the family. Lord Nairne died in 1726, his son John could not succeed to the title but he did obtain the right to inherit property and lived at the House of Nairne with his mother and family until the Clans came out again in 1745, when he immediately rejoined his Jacobite friends. The defeat of Culloden meant that once more the Nairnes lost their property and this time they went abroad. Lady Nairne died at Versailles in 1754, and was buried in the Protestant Cemetery near the Port St. Martin, in Paris. In 1764 the Duke of Atholl destroyed what remained of the House of Nairne, having previously removed everything of value and sold the timber on the estate. Four years later The Hon. John Nairne, *de jure* third Baron, died in France at the age of 79. Thus was extinguished a hardy and obdurate race of men (and women) loyal and true, when all trace of their earthly bodies and works had been removed.

In striking contrast to this story of the unfortunate but steadfast Nairnes is that of the Hopes of Hopetoun, whose first ennobled representative commissioned Bruce to build Hopetoun House, and who, twenty years afterwards, at the instigation of his artist brother-in-law' had the whole thing pulled to pieces, or at any rate transformed and enlarged, to suit more affluent tastes at the hands of William Adam of Maryburgh. In between the first building and the second, Sir William Bruce then seventy eight, was called back to build the elaborate laird's loft in Abercorn Parish Kirk, about a mile away on the edge of the deer park, with its adjacent Burial Aisle and elegant retiring rooms above for the new Earl.

The site is suggestive to a degree, the old Kirk is in part built on the foundations of a very early Scottish Cathedral founded in Celtic times, the chancel retains, in the main, the masonic shell of a medieval structure; while diggings in the vicinity have brought to light the remnants of monastic quarters long since emptied and reduced to mere footings. At the Reformation, or later, under the 1689 Presbyterian dispensation, the seating and liturgical arrangements in the church were altered, so that instead of facing the Holy Table the pews were re-orientated in a north to south position, facing sideways onto the former chancel and across the body of the church with the pulpit as focal point. Thus the east end became vacant, so to speak, and accordingly the Earl of Hopetoun appropriated it to his own ends, commissioning Bruce to build across it a magnificent gallery, or Loft, where he and his family could sit looking down upon the congregation but not, as at present, in full view of them. The term box is, really, more appropriate than loft, for this is in essence an 'opera box,' richly carved and panelled, with the Earl's Achievement painted in full heraldic tinctures behind. It resembles nothing so much as the Royal Box in the Cathedral at Turin, installed there by the Sicilian architect Fillipo Iuvara for the benefit of members of the House of Savoy whose Duke acquired Royal status in 1713. [4]

The contract and accounts for the Hopetoun loft are extant and show that the very elaborate and fine carving, and notably the freize along the front facing the Church (with its mixture of heraldic and natural forms intermingled in the Continental baroque manner) was done by William Eizat, a member of the same gifted family Bruce employed at Holyrood, Kinross, and elsewhere, and notably at Hopetoun House itself. The splendid Achievement on the back of the coomb ceiling was painted by Richard Waitt, a contemporary Scottish portrait painter, two of whose works, a self-portrait and an early rendering of a Scottish Chieftain in full Highland regalia (Kenneth, Third Lord Duffus) may be seen in the Scottish National Portrait Gallery in Edinburgh, the self-portrait being on loan. Until recently the panelling and carving was all, without discrimination, covered in the most awful dark stain, to make it look like oak I suppose, when it is in fact excellent Memel pine. Now, however, the stain has been removed, the carving picked out in full colours, the panelling painted French grey and the ceiling left the *bleu de ciel* it, fortunately, already was.

There is no way into the church from the loft, or vice versa, and the only entrance is from the park, up stairs that climb to the first floor above the burial vault. Here one finds oneself in a handsome panelled lobby, with the usual lugged architraves to the doors, a coombed ceiling and beyond, straight ahead, is the laird's loft, or gallery. A door on the right leads to one large and one small retiring room and a privy. The latter still has its original wooden seat and hole for bucket and must be one of the oldest in the country. The large retiring room has been done out in the same blue-green as the principal bedroom at Auchendinny and the Long Gallery at Holyrood; the Corinthian pilasters on either side of the moulded stone chimneypiece and scrolled bases to the panelling should have been touched up with gold but with a Ministry Grant only the sheerest necessities were either practicable or permissable.

The small retiring room is in its way the *piece de resistance,* or at least it was before the Victorians turned the seats in the kirk back to the west to east position, re-clothed both nave and what was left of the chancel in mock-Norman, and erected altar steps where no altar stood. This meant that the floor level in the vestry had to be raised, bringing the ceiling up through the floor of the small retiring room above. The Victorians did other stupid things, such as erecting a tubular bell-set on the outside gable end of the church to commemorate Queen Victoria's Jubilee. They even took away the fine Georgian pulpit and sounding board. More reprehensibly they blocked up the large oval squint between the small retiring room and the church, which was the whole point of the room, for through this opening the Hopes were able to see from a safe distance whether or not the Minister was in his pulpit, and if so would come through into their loft from the large retiring room to hear the sermon. You see, they used to spend the whole sabbath in the Kirk or the Aisle, hearing one sermon in the morning and another in the afternoon, taking cold collation in the larger retiring room at mid-day, and warming themselves there betimes. Happily the Historic Buildings Council insisted on the re-opening of the old squint which Bruce built for his Hope clients in 1708. It has had to be glazed, of course, though it never was before, otherwise the Minister would be blown out of his pulpit, but the entire arrangements and design, only slightly modified, is unrivalled in these islands. There are quite a few laird's lofts in Scotland and elaborate and comfortable family pews exist in various parts of England, but nothing quite like this; and surely no similar squint room?

The Aisle is virtually a separate structure from the church and loft, though there is a small physical junction. Its hipped, bell-cast roof, moulded cornice, limewashed walls and plain rustications stand out in striking contrast to the romantically gabled east end of the kirk proper, replete with the odd remnant of a Romanesque arch imbedded in gothic masonry, and a King's head or two sticking out as corbels. Bruce had to make the best of a rather awkward and unusual juxtaposition of architectural styles, and did so by keeping the front of his classically inspired addition right away from the old church, creating a formal, semi-circular approach from the park side with curving side wings, niches and ornamental finials (the latter have since been redistributed and now adorn other gateposts on the Hopetoun estate). The architect evidently remained faithful to the last to those principles of symmetry, proportion and taste which he had tried out so successfully more than a quarter of a century earlier at Balcaskie.

1 One is reminded of Thomas Carlyle's observations on Chelsea Hospital, designed by Bruce's English contemporary, Sir Christopher Wren. 'It has always given me pleasure to see it,' he reflected, 'I saw that it was quiet and dignified and the work of a *gentleman*.'

2 This is nearly as much as the first estimate for the rebuilding of Holyrood-house.

3 Bishop Forbes in his *Journal* mentions a visit made in 1762 to the ruins of the "modern House of Nairn," and especially noted the Chapel, which had been consecrated in 1713 by Bishop Rose of Edinburgh. The Duke of Atholl demolished what was left two years later.

4 Victor Amadeus, whose spouse was Anne d'Orleans, daughter of Charles I's "Minette," and neice of Charles II.

Wemysshall, Fife (now rebuilt)

CHAPTER NINE

Quasi-Bruce and non-Bruce

SIR WILLIAM BRUCE of Kinross, Bart, died in 1710, still in architectural harness and only just out of protective custody in Edinburgh Castle. The last published letter to him contains in its opening sentence the writer's astonishment that this grand old man remained in close confinement, though it appears he was definitely released before his death. Whilst yet in prison, however, he resigned the hereditary Sheriffdom of 'Kinrosher' in favour of his son, and in 1711, when Sir John Bruce died without heirs, the whole estate and perquisites thereto passed to Anne Bruce, the architect's daughter, known locally as 'Lady Kinross.' She in turn died shortly afterwards in 1715, and was succeeded by her eldest son, Thomas. In the same year occurred one of the first of several fortunate circumstances whereby Kinross House was spared possible damage and forfeiture, thus coming down to us virtually unaltered 'since its completion about 1695. In 1715 Sir Thomas Bruce Hope of Kinross, acting in his capacity as Sheriff of the County, formally proclaimed James VIII and III at the Mercat Cross of the Burgh, with the result that his house and land stood in immediate danger of confiscation at the hands of the victorious Hanoverians. However, when a party of government troops led by the Earl of Rothes (his kinsman) arrived, Colonel John Hope, Sir Thomas's heir and brother, took the precautionary step of arresting the Jacobite laird, so saving Kinross House from sequestration and probable sale and demolition, as happened at the House of Nairne. He posted two dragoons (members of Tam Dalyell's famous Scots Greys) at the gates, and rode down the long avenue alone to take charge of his brother, who at that moment was trying, with the assistance of the head gardener, to escape via the 'Fish Gate.'

The Sheriffdom was transferred to Colonel Hope, Kinross House and lands were spared an attainder, and when a repentant, re-instated Sir Thomas died in 1729, brother John became laird and fourth

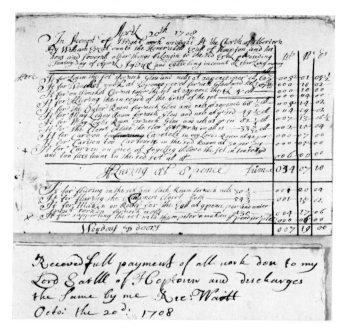

91 Receipts from Wm. Eizat for joinerwork and
Richard Waitt for painting done at Abercorn in 1708

92 Detail richly carved freize by Wm. Eizat and
the first Earl of Hopetoun's Achievement painted by
Richard Waitt

93 Looking from the retiring room through the squint to the church at Abercorn

94   Detail chimneypiece and panelling in retiring room after restoration

95   Sir William Bruce in old age by Sir John de Medina. Portrait at
       Holyrood on loan from the Scottish National Portrait Gallery

baronet. He had had an interesting career, first in the army of the Duke of Marlborough, then as Governor of Bermuda. He was Member of Parliament for 'Kinrosher' between 1723 and 1734, and again between 1741 and '47. He died in 1766, all his children having predeceased him, so that the property passed to James Carstairs, only son of Anne Bruce and her second husband, Sir John Carstairs of Kilconquhar. In 1768 the new Carstairs laird died and his son James, after disposing of the Tailzie, or entail, by Act of Parliament, sold Kinross to George Graham, retired East Indian Merchant, an ancestor in the female line of the present laird, Sir David Montgomery of Kinross, Bart.

Many of the valauble furnishings and pictures mentioned by Defoe and others as being in Kinross House were disposed of in 1777, the rest went in 1819, on the demise of George Graham's son, Thomas, the sale then lasting more than a week and raising nearly £4000. It was during the tenancy of Thomas Graham that the house survived, almost without scaith, a second serious crisis in its history, for it was this same Thomas Graham who, having removed Bruce's 'Great Dorick Gate,' proceeded to try and eradicate all the decoration on the facade of the house itself, but was foiled by the good folk of Kinross. Until Sir Basil Montgomery came to live at Kinross the place stood empty, and was thus spared for a third time what might have been, a cultural disaster, for who can doubt that Victorian occupants could not have resisted the temptation to enlarge or otherwise mutilate Sir William Bruce's noble, but for them, over plain house? Sir Basil restored it to its former glory and also replaced its missing or displaced parts as near as he could to Bruce's original drawings and plans. What a pity these did not include the gates; but they did not, and lacking even written descriptions supposition had to take the place of known or recorded fact. The result is excellent and in perfect taste, but there is no proof that it represents what the first Scottish architect, the Scottish Inigo Jones, drew for Tobias Bauchop or made a model of nearly two-and-a-half centuries before.[1]

One of Sir William Bruce's pupils was, of course, William Adam of Maryburgh, father of the celebrated Adam Brothers, but his style developed quite differently, displaying a penchant for extravagant Roman baroque forms which would have dismayed the reticent and genuinely aristocratic Baronet of Kinross. Much more in the Bruce manner were the works of James Smith of Whytehill, now the estate of Newhailes, near Musselburgh, who seems to have been the principal inspiration for Colen Campbell's deserting Law for the 'Mistress Art,' and whose Palladian drawings, many of them recording well known buildings in the Inigo Jones style in England, have, until now, been confused with those of Campbell, his disciple. In fact, a recent purchase by the R.I.B.A. of drawings attributed to Colen Campbell has revealed this very point, and the Curator at the Royal Institute now thinks that Smith may be the veritable 'missing link', between the earlier efforts of Jones and his pupils in Jacobean and Caroline England, and the resumption of the Palladian ideals in the first half of the eighteenth century; when Campbell's *Vitruvius Britannicus* came out and had so pronounced an effect on taste.

Principal architectural link in all this was, probably, the Castle of Drumlanrig, in Dumfriesshire, which appears in the British *Vitruvius* though completed before Campbell's emergence on the scene. It was begun before the Restoration, held up, then recommenced in 1679 and finished in 1689. Both Bruce and Smith were participants, the fomer giving advice, the latter acting as agent between Bruce and the Duke of Queensberry in arranging exchanges of craftsmen from Kinross. Drumlanrig is a close copy of Heriot's Hospital, in Edinburgh, in the initial stages of which Inigo Jones himself is said to have had a hand, indeed, both under James VI and I, and again under Charles I, Jones is traditionally supposed to have visited the Scottish Capital and assisted in various restorations and new buildings. The West Door of the Abbey Kirk at Holyrood, for instance, is often quoted as having been designed by him. In any event there is a connection of some sort, and this certainly comes out in the 'show' front at Drumlanrig, where the admixture of Renaissance and Gothic, if not quite 'a poor mixture of the classic and the grotesque' as stated in the *DNB*, clearly shows a most picturesque and naïve use of the Palladian elements that has no equal in the North, possibly not in Britain. The entrance steps *au fer a cheval* are clearly derived from those at the Queen's House, Greenwich, and were later adapted by William Adam at the main entrance to Duff House, Banffshire, his masterpiece; and the *tout ensemble*, mammoth 'orders,' heavy pediments, rich heraldic carving, base-course arcading and crowning ducal coronet (copied from the Royal Crown and cupola at Holyrood) are almost overwhelming in their theatrical effect, at least when seen at a little distance. *MacGibbon and Ross*, the usual source when seeking information on earlier Scottish castles and houses, says that the architect of Drumlanrig is unknown, but that the mason's name was Lukup, a statement that can easily be corroborated by a visit to the village churchyard at Durisdeer, where a gravestone describes William Lukup as 'Master of Works in Drumlanrig 1685.' Nearby, in the ogee roofed Aisle of the Dukes of Queensberry are the famous 'Queensberry Marbles,' a typically profuse Van Nost tribute in black-and-white to a wealthy patron and his lady, the latter 'being sprung on the father's side from the

112

illustrious families of Burlington and Cumberland.' I do not know if Lukup also built the late-classical Aisle, probably not, but James Smith may have. He was also the architect of Dalkeith Palace, completed about the same time as Drumlanrig for the widowed Duchess of Monmouth and Buccleuch. Smith's name has been associated with another contemporary mansion of note, Melville House, in Fife, where Bruce's advice, as elsewhere, was sought periodically, though he does not appear to have designed the building as such. It is too plain and unadorned in any case, and lacks those individual touches, those patrician details one always associates with him, and which never fail to occur even in his smallest works.

The late Sir Stirling Maxwell, K.T., a founder member of the Royal Commission on Ancient Monuments in Scotland, thought very highly of Melville and writes at length about it in his *Shrines and Homes of Scotland*. There is a fine photograph in the book of the place as it was before being sold to become a boy's school. There is much to remind one of Bruce, the sense of proportion, the simple use of good, wholesome materials, handsome and well placed chimneys, lugged architraves to the windows, rusticated quoins, central cupola and gentle bell-cast roof. Not to mention an early use of pedimented centrepieces, on the east and west elevations, the usual side wings and gazebos, urns and enclosed forecourt. A miniature version of Melville, at Raith, overlooking the Firth of Forth above Kirkcaldy, was begun for the Earl of Melville's son and heir, Lord Raith, Treasurer Depute of Scotland in succession to Lord Hatton, about 1692. Here again both Bruce and Smith seem to have had a hand in the building. Raith has a very fine and expansive pedimented entrance feature with some expressive baroque carving ready to take a cartouche of the owner's Coat of Arms but now filled with a successor's Coat, the remnants of curving side-wings and some rebuilt side pavilions. It was probably begun by Bruce and finished by Smith, about the same time the latter commenced work at Melville, in 1697. Raith has been considerably altered since. Lord Raith died without an heir and the place was sold to a Kirkcaldy merchant named Ferguson whose successors have spent much money on the house and made considerable enlargements, so that inside practically the only survivals of the earlier period are a handsome back stair rail, very likely the work of James Horn of Kirkcaldy (who did the wrought-iron work at Kinross), part of an elaborate plaster ceiling and a few late-Stewart chimneypieces.

Melville, on the other hand, has stood intact ever since its first occupation and furnishing at the turn of the seventeenth and eighteenth centuries, even to such items as the table linen and minor household necessities, the inventory, as at Ham, being there to check.

The plain exterior was matched by one of the richest interiors in the country, though all but the actual fixtures, panelling and chimney-pieces, were bought in the south and sent up specially. The contents were sold recently, including the magnificent *lit de parade*, but the panelling remains, and the splendid staircase, and, of course, the architecture of the house itself has remained unchanged, though adapted to another purpose. Sir John Stirling Maxwell's comments in general, therefore, are still applicable, and typical of Bruce, and quasi-Bruce houses. Of it he says : 'The house is large, but no house could be more compact or more comfortable. In summer it is deliciously cool, in winter so warm that a rudimentary stove below the great staircase supplies all the central heating required. On such perfection there can be little advance, and in fact there has been none except in the matter of bathrooms and lifts. Though the house stands under a hill its chimneys have never been disgraced by a chimney pot. This can be said of few buildings except those of Wren, whose Chelsea Hospital is, in this respect, such a contrast to its neighbours in London.' It is evident from this that James Smith and his associates learned well at the feet of Sir William Bruce and obviously took his advice seriously.

The author of *Homes and Shrines* (in the 1937 edition) goes on to attribute the gateways and garden houses at Pollock Castle, near Glasgow, to Bruce, but although the gazebos in question have characteristic ogee roofs and the gateways are delightfully classical in the French manner there is no documentary proof for this connection, and I am afraid we must accept them as from an unknown hand. Their accomplished appearance certainly suggests a 'master,' and they are too imaginatively decorated to be by the chaste Mr Smith; but the main gate at Pollock is virtually a copy of one at Hatton, erstwhile home of our old friend Charles Maitland, brother of the Duke of Lauderdale and third Earl. We do not know for certain who designed Hatton itself, it may have been the Treasurer Depute and newly appointed Surveyor to the King personally, or he may have had the nerve to pick Sir William Bruce's brains, and then rely on using the same craftsmen as were employed at Holyrood. Whatever did happen, Hatton too has gone, and in the same decade as Moncreiffe, Panmure and Craighall. Only a forlorn looking gazebo and an old turreted tower, plus the handsome baroque gate, remain to tell the tale. The gate, incidentally, now considerably knocked about and in some danger of collapse, or removal, bears the inscription ANNO DOM 1692, on one side, and 1829 on the other, a reference to its placing here when the original avenue to the house was cut down and a new entry made.

The interior of Hatton was the equal of Holyrood, as well it might be knowing the originator, while the exterior, grouped around an older structure, had a large court in front with ogee roofed pavilions at the corners. There was also a bath house, and a bowling green with a classical pavilion, it is this that remains. There is a fine 'aerial view' of Hatton House in Slezer's *Theatrum Scotiae* showing how much the designer, whoever he was, owed to Sir William Bruce. It has not, however, ever been directly attributed to him. Caroline Park, a contemporary structure, has, on the other hand, and it, like Hatton, was partly built with government funds and craftsmen sent from Holyrood by a holder of high office, Viscount Tarbet, later first Earl of Cromartie, Justice-General and Secretary of State for Scotland. Under the name of Royston, this 'cottage' (really a large mansion) was built by the Tarbets, George and Anna Mackenzie, 'for our comfort and that of our friends.' I can find absolutely no evidence that Sir William Bruce had anything positive to do with Royston (renamed Caroline Park in the eighteenth century after both Queen Caroline and the eldest daughter of the then owner, the second Duke of Argyll). I have searched all the relevant records, even enquired of the present Earl of Cromartie, but nowhere can I discover a documented Bruce connection, not even a loose one, as at Drumlanrig, Melville and Raith.

Apart from the lack of substantive evidence, there are also certain stylistic objections to any close association between Bruce and Royston (Caroline Park), objections which are actually more apparent there than at Hatton, for although parts of the house, and especially the older, northern wing and the interior, repeat things reminiscent of what he did at Holyrood,[2] the main, south facade, completed in 1696, completely lacks that refinement of detail for which the King's Architect was known. Furthermore, although there are the usual elaborate fretwork ceilings, splendid wrought-iron stair rails, fine panelling, even the occasional corner fireplace, much of this was by craftsmen other than those known to Bruce, though, naturally, a number of them had worked for him. The painted ceilings and inset panels, for example, were not done by his favourite Dutchmen but by French artists, including Nicolas de Heude, whose signature appears on the ceiling of the saloon. He was an assistant of Antonio Verrio, better known for his work at Hampton Court and at Windsor. Other features are cruder than anything Bruce would have permitted. Though boldly executed they lack his restraint and sense of proportion. *MacGibbon and Ross* is of the same opinion, and so is Mr Henry Kerr, whose articles on the life and work of Sir William Bruce of Kinross in the *Quarterly of the Royal Incorporation of Architects in Scotland* for 1924/25 have been referred to previously. Neither includes Caroline Park in their list of Bruce houses, though he is thought to have been 'an interested party,' presumably because some of the tradesmen engaged there were folk with whom he wished to keep in touch.

There is another, more important objection, however, to the suggestion that Bruce played a significant part in the design of Caroline Park, at least its 1696 re-facing, which is after all, the most remarkable feature of the whole house. This was added at a time when Tarbet, having made his peace with the new 'Government of William-anmary,' had embarked upon a fresh and successful post-revolution career. In 1696 Sir William Bruce was imprisoned for his lukewarm reception of the revolutionary settlement, and one can scarcely imagine him being employed then by a powerful agent of that settlement to build a country house for him. While as for Royston's noble southern facade, that is unique in Scotland. It not only does not resemble any known work of Bruce's but is unlike any other work by any other Scottish architect of the period. In fact, it is a rough copy of a portion of the Château of Champ-de-Bataille, in Normandy, which building is thought to be a rustic essay in the style of François le Vau, younger brother of the renowned Louis le Vau, architect of Vaux-le-Vicomte. It rather looks as if Tarbet was familiar with Champ-de-Bataille, or, since there were French craftsmen at work in the house, one of them designed the Royston facade from memory.

I have spent some time on this little known example of a quasi-Bruce house because it is the most evocative and best preserved of its kind in Scotland. It was the childhood home of Henry Cockburn, eminent judge and part founder of Britain's oldest amenity society. It was also, until 1966, the property of an ink manufacturing firm who treated the place with the utmost respect, until it became too small and inconvenient for their purposes, when they were able to sell it back to the Duke of Buccleuch, whose ancestors were the owners in the late eighteenth and nineteenth centuries. Though not really a 'Bruce House,' Caroline Park could not have been conceived without his example. He was so esteemed an architect, especially in Scotland, that it is only natural that proprietors of 'Bruce Houses,' authenticated or otherwise, are generally tremendously proud of the association, much more so than with most other architect designed houses. William Adam has his supporters, and many of the non-Bruce houses, the majority I would say, are labelled 'Adam' in a general sort of way, whether they were by William Adam or not. None of the Adam family, however, even the father who was trained in the Bruce tradition, can be said to have continued his style, though the Scottish genius for architecture (an art in which a love of phantasy is matched by an almost equal love of order and logic) was as strong in them as in their Palladian forerunners, Bruce and Smith.

William Adam's *Vitruvius Scoticus* shows drawings of Holyrood, Kinross, Mertoun, Rothes, Panmure, Craighill and other houses designed by Sir William Bruce, and also one, Elie House, in Fife, which Adam claims for himself. Elie is actually thought locally to be a 'Bruce House,' I have seen this stated in the *'East Neuk Press'* and also, though not absolutely definitely, in the Rev. W. Wood's *East Neuk of Fife its History and Antiquities*, wherein also will be found the information that Elie House was built for Sir William Anstruther of that Ilk in 1697. I paid a visit to it recently and the whole atmosphere of the place is 'Adam,' father Adam, old 'lime and mortar' as he was called, though I am willing to admit that Sir William Bruce may have systematized, if one can use such a word, the original laird's tower, presumably in 1697, and that either Smith or Smith's partner, Alexander Macgill (architect to Edinburgh Corporation and later, with Smith, co-designer of Yester House, for the Marquis of Tweedale) had something to do with the garden facade. Yester, curiously enough, was completed by William and Robert Adam, so perhaps that is what happened at Elie too?

Although James Smith was Bruce's chief assistant at Holyrood, and eventually inherited his 'master's' official post, in many respects the truest disciple of the 'Scottish Inigo Jones' was Colen Campbell, who was probably brought to architecture by Smith. It is a pity, therefore, that nothing of Campbell's has survived North of the Border, if indeed he ever built anything in his native land, for it would, I feel sure, have helped us solve a great deal that must at present remain conjectural, both as regards Campbell's own career and the way in which Palladianism spread, first from Jones to Bruce, then from Bruce via Smith and Campbell to influence the works of Sir William Chambers and Charles Cameron. William Adam and his family rather broke away from this particular tradition, as did James Gibbs, who was Wren's follower and the protégè of that Earl of Mar who spent his days in exile planning the New Town of Edinburgh. Mar sent Gibbs to Rome, whence he returned to Britain a confirmed Roman Baroque architect, not a Palladian. A lot of Colen Campbell's designs, on the other hand, do show a touch of Bruce, and are certainly Palladian. Of course, he knew Sir William Bruce's principal houses, and Hopetoun, his most mature, appears in *Vitruvius Britannicus*, together with Drumlanrig and Melville, works in which Bruce and Smith were jointly associated. Thus it will be doubly interesting, when the "Smith Drawings," accepted for two centuries as all Campbell's, have been fully examined and assessed, to see just exactly what part he and Bruce played in the development and dissemination of Palladian ideas in Britain, North and South, in late Stewart times.

¹ The entrance gates at Newbattle Abbey, Midlothian, designed by Bruce's successor and former assistant, James Smith, do, however, suggest a possible design, including as they do two lions, on either side of the posts, and various other Kinross-like features.

² There are distinct affinities between the courtyard plans adopted at Holyrood, Drumlanrig and Caroline Park, and in the galleried centrepieces at Hatton, Prestonfield, features which Bruce himself broke completely away from at Kinross and Hopetoun, Moncreiff and Mertoun, and which do not occur at Melville or Raith.

Hatton House (now demolished)

Appendices

Visiting buildings designed by Sir William Bruce

BALCASKIE, Fife (Sir Ralph Anstruther Bart). Bruce's first house is not normally open to the public though once a year, usually in July, the gardens are on view under 'Scotland's Garden Scheme.'

HOLYROODHOUSE, Edinburgh (H.M. The Queen). The Palace is usually open to the public except when Her Majesty the Queen is in residence or during the period of the General Assembly of the Church of Scotland (the third week in May). An illustrated guide is available which, however, is largely devoted to romantic history and legend and the name of the royal architect of this splendid place is not even mentioned; though recently the Long Gallery has been redecorated and completed as he designed it and his portrait, by Sir John de Medina, hangs on the staircase, on loan from the National Portrait Gallery of Scotland.

PRESTONFIELD HOUSE, Edinburgh (Mrs Janet Dick-Cunyngham). This beautiful house, still in the possession of a descendant of the original builders, is run as an hotel, and can easily be seen by those who patronise it. Rich chimneypieces, leather hangings and ornate fret-work ceilings, the work of the same craftsmen who built Holyroodhouse under Sir Wm. Bruce remain *in situ*.

THIRLESTANE CASTLE, Berwickshire (The Dowager Countess of Lauderdale). Thirlestane, remodelled after Ham for the Duke and Duchess of Lauderdale, whose Scottish seat it was, is on view to interested persons by appointment, and during the summer on special days under 'Scotland's Garden's Scheme' and other officially organised tours.

KINROSS HOUSE, Kinross-shire (Mrs P. R. Montgomery). Bruce's masterpiece and the finest formed garden in Scotland are on view only by special appointment, though official parties run by the National Trust for Scotland and other bodies do visit Kinross on occasion. The gardens are open under 'Scotland's Gardens Scheme,' usually in August.

MERTOUN HOUSE, Berwickshire (The Duke of Sutherland). Mertoun, originally the House of Harden and built by Bruce for a kinsman of his second wife, is not normally open to the public, though once a year, usually in the late summer, the grounds are on view under 'Scotland's Gardens Scheme.'

THE OLD TOLBOOTH, Stirling (The Town Clerk, Municipal Buildings). This is open to the public by special appointment, and contains several panelled rooms of the Bruce period. The exterior is easily seen from the street.

AUCHENDINNY HOUSE, Midlothian (John D. McCulloch Esq.). Bruce's last design is only open under special circumstances and usually once a year under 'Scotland's Gardens Scheme.' It is very charming and one of the very few 'Queen Anne' country houses north of the border. A fine *coup d'oeil* may be had from the Edinburgh Leadburn Road shortly after Milton Bridge.

HOPETOUN HOUSE AND THE HOPE AISLE ABERCORN, West Lothian (The Marquis of Linlithgow MC). Hopetoun, sometimes called 'The Versailles of Scotland' is still basically a Sir William Bruce House, though with an Adam front and side wings. It is open to the public every day except Thursdays and Fridays, from the end of April until the beginning of October. Besides the State Rooms, many of them designed by Bruce, visitors are shown the museum which contains the original contract for the building of the house with the signatures of Sir William Bruce and the first Earl of Hopetoun's representatives, the Earl himself being a minor at the time. The park was laid out by Bruce and the garden facade remains as he designed it. The guide book has an interesting juxtaposition of plans showing Bruce's original layout with the Adam family's additions superimposed. The ballroom serves as a large tearoom and shop. The Hope Aisle, completed in 1708 to Bruce's design and by the same workmen who built the house, lies across the park and is attached to the east end of Abercorn Kirk. Permission to view, when the Church is closed, may be had from the Parish Minister, at the Manse. The Aisle has recently been restored and the panelling painted and coloured as it would have been in the first decade of the 18th century. Included are the Hope family's retiring rooms and gallery, with Richard Waitt's splendid Armorial Achievement above.

Other buildings.

Of the other buildings associated with Sir Wm. Bruce but not conclusively his, Drumlanrig Castle, Raith House, Caroline Park and Melville House only the last named can be visited, by special permission of the headmaster. On the other hand it may be worth the reader's while going to see some of the more important houses known to Bruce in his youth, both in England and France, some of which are open to the public. A short list is appended below, with details of visiting arrangements.

HAM HOUSE, Richmond (The National Trust). This was the London home of the Duke and Duchess of Lauderdale, Bruce's principal private patrons, the Duchess being his cousin. It is open to the public every day except Mondays, Christmas Day and Good Friday, and should be visited on several accounts. A young Sir William Bruce designed the Gates, but more than this the interior is almost exactly as furnished and decorated in 1679 when the first inventory was made, and the gardens have been restored to something approaching their Caroline splendour. John Evelyn thought them the finest in England though a traveller to Scotland towards the end of the 17th century remarked that Bruce's gardens at Kinross 'made Lady Lauderdale's at Ham but a wilderness by comparison.' The Chapel is of special interest since the interior of Lauder Kirk, in Berwickshire, Bruce's only complete ecclesiastical design, has been completely altered. Here all the contemporary liturgical fittings have remained *in situ*.

VAUX-LE-VICOMTE, Maincy, Seine-et-Marne, France (Madame Sommier). No thorough understanding of what Bruce was trying to do at Kinross can be obtained without a visit to Fouquet's great chateau at Vaux-le-Vicomte. This, the first of the really grand designs of the period, was completed in 1661, when Bruce was making one of his trips to France, and there can be no doubt that what he saw there influenced his work at home. The Grounds are open at weekends from Palm Sunday to Armistice Day (Nov. 11th), and if one writes to Madame Sommier permission is usually given to view the interior on some other day.

BLOIS, Loir-et-Cher, France (Owned by the State). The former royal chateau at Blois is one of the best known in the Valley of the Loire and is open throughout the year. The Gaston d'Orleans wing, in which F. Mansart employed the three orders of architecture so expertly, was completed in 1638, and probably served to guide Sir William Bruce in his design of the Courtyard at Holyroodhouse.

BALLEROY, Calvados, France (The Marquis de Choisy). The chateau was completed by Mansart about 1636, and should be visited by anyone who is holidaying in Normandy. Like Ham it remains largely as originally designed and furnished and was one of the buildings that Bruce probably knew. Of especial interest are the side wings and pavilions, the central cupola and general symmetry of the layout of gardens and park. The entry from the village along an avenue of trees that continues the same line as the house in the street is noteworthy.

BLERANCOURT, Aisne, France (Franco-American Friendship Committee). This Chateau contains a Museum of Franco-American friendship and is open every day of the year. Only a small portion of the principal buildings survives but the original garden pavilions and formal layout designed by Salomon de Brosse in the reign of Louis XIII remain and are decidedly worth a detour. Sir William Bruce cannot fail to have seen these and the ogee-roofed side pavilions have several echoes north of the border. Salomon de Brosse was architect to the king's mother, Marie de Medicis and whilst in Paris one should go and look at the Fontaine de Medicis in the Luxembourg Gardens, with its *congelations* and other watery, rustic features that clearly are reflected in 'The Fishgate' at Kinross.

Gazebo, Hopetoun

What to Read

It is surprising how few reliable books there are on the subject of Scottish Architecture, and how late in time the gap is gradually being filled. The latest, *Architecture of Scotland*, by George Hay, a useful compendium but extremely concise, only appeared in the summer of 1969, while the very first comprehensive volume of modern times, John G. Dunbar's *The Historic Architecture of Scotland*, was published by Batsford as recently as 1966. At that time the draft of *Architect Royal* had already been completed, so that there was virtually nothing of a general nature to go on at all, unless one went back to original documents and half-finished manuscripts. The late Mr David Marshall, who tidied up the Charter Room at Kinross, published some extremely useful notes in Volume 14 of the Society of Antiquaries in Scotland, and these may be seen in the Register House in Edinburgh. More easily obtainable are the relevant copies of the *Quarterly* magazine of the Royal Incorporation of Architects in Scotland (1924), in which the architectural historian, Mr H. F. Kerr, dealt with a number of Bruce buildings and attempted to list his achievements, while the Volumes of *Castellated and Domestic Architecture of Scotland* by MacGibbon and Ross are frequently come by. In them brief mention will be found of the place of Sir William Bruce in the rise of Palladian Architecture in the north plus details of Craighall, in Fife, and some of the neo-Bruce structures such as Drumlanrig Castle and Caroline Park. A particularly well written and informative booklet is the *Guide to Ham House* by Ralph Edwards and Peter Ward-Jackson published by the Stationery Office for the Victoria & Albert Museum. This does not mention Bruce as such but gives a great deal of detail on his cousin the Countess of Dysart, afterwards Duchess of Lauderdale, and about the furnishings in that splendid Charles II mansion which Sir William Bruce knew so well. There is a lot more about the Lauderdales and their part in assisting Bruce's career in the late Rev. Robert Mylne's *Master Masons to the Crown of Scotland*, which is really an edited version of the Mylne Papers, in which is documented the building of Holyroodhouse. A useful little book of pre-war vintage is *Stones of Scotland*, edited by George Scott Moncrieff with contributions by the late Mr Douglas Simpson and Ian G. Lindsay. The Chapter 'Triumphant Classicism' by Ian C. Hannah is particularly worth reading. Finally, the archives of *Country Life Ltd.* are as always rewarding, and in 1954 they published *Scottish Country Houses and Gardens open to the public*, by John Fleming. One only wishes that this most attractively produced book could be relied upon in all its details, both as regards the houses actually open to the public and their histories. Amongst the more obvious errors when dealing with Sir William Bruce are two, one in which the author describes the King's Architect as, 'a wiry, ginger-headed Scot with sharp eyes and an air of self-confidence which evidently served him well in his political career,' and another in which he ascribes the show-front of Drumlanrig positively to Bruce, though there are no definite grounds for this. Bruce was, of course, neither wiry nor ginger-headed, though he may have had an air of self-confidence. He was dark and swarthy as his portrait shows. However, these and other details apart, the general background writing does stimulate an interest in Scottish Architecture, and in this book will be found, besides notes and views on Kinross, Drumlanrig and Thirlestane, an excellent piece on Hopetoun. The best article, or rather articles, on Kinross to date were written by Mr Mark Girouard and published in *Country Life* in their issues of March 25th., and April 1st., 1965 respectively. Finally a short film on the life and works of Sir William Bruce has recently been made by Park Studios, Glasgow, for 'Educational Films of Scotland'. This is in colour and has a spoken commentary, and although produced with Government help and primarily intended for schools and colleges is also available at a modest fee to societies and other interested parties. Details from the Secretary, Educational Films of Scotland, 16/17 Woodside Terrace, Glasgow C.3.

Shrines and Homes of Scotland, by the way, which I have referred to in the text and in which there are a number of comments anent the work of Sir William Bruce, was written by the late Sir John Stirling Maxwell almost in desperation, since there was not at that time, 1937, any book in existence which gave a good general picture of Scottish Architecture. Latter day research has made some of Sir John's comments slightly out of date, but his book nevertheless remains an inspiring and provoking introduction to a subject that still needs a great deal more exploring. I'm glad to say that it has been re-issued and is still on the bookstands.

Bridgegate Steeple, Glasgow

Gates to Kinross (rebuilt early 20th century)

Index

THIRLESTANE